What
EXCEPTIONAL
EXECUTIVES
Need to Know

ELIZABETH JEFFRIES

What Exceptional Executives Need to Know
Your Step-by-Step Coaching Guide to Busting Communication Barriers,
Keeping Top Talent & *Growing Your Emerging Leaders!*
By Elizabeth Jeffries

Designed, produced, and published by SPARK Publications
SPARKpublications.com
Charlotte, NC 28227

Printing History:
Edition One, January 2018, ISBN 978-1-943070-27-5

Library of Congress Control Number: 2017958994

BUS071000 BUSINESS & ECONOMICS / Leadership
BUS041000 BUSINESS & ECONOMICS / Management

Praise for
What Exceptional Executives Need to Know

"Elizabeth Jeffries is a hall of fame speaker and a highly sought-after executive coach because of her experience, enthusiasm, and dedication to her clients. In *What Exceptional Executives Need to Know* you'll not only find step-by-step procedures on how to get results, but through her real-life executive development encounters you'll see and feel how you can recreate her magic with your own team members."

– PETER J. ADAMO, President/CEO, Waterbury Hospital

"Elizabeth Jeffries shares her 'secret sauce' through inspirational stories that help illustrate how we can help ourselves and other leaders master their gifts – heart, mind, and soul. If you are looking for a proven method and holistic approach to coach leaders on your team and in your organization, *What Exceptional Executives Need to Know* is a must-read."

– DR. JEAN ANN LARSON, FACHE, LFHIMSS, FIISE, DSHS, Leadership Development Officer, University of Alabama at Birmingham – Health System and School of Medicine

"Elizabeth Jeffries has created an excellent roadmap in this book for leaders to help them coach their team, to bring out the very best in each person resulting in performance excellence. This well-written book provides you with the principles of coaching and how to put on the 'Coach's Crown' and use the 5 Cs of communicating to lead and develop dynamic, thought-provoking discussions. You'll learn what it means to speak the 'truth in love' in order for coaching to be effective. You owe it to yourself to read this book!"

– LISA MORLEY, Vice President - Human Resources, First Savings Bank

"Elizabeth Jeffries imparts her years of experience in the often-neglected art of executives as coach to their team members. In this ideal guide for stretching your coaching muscles, she shares her wisdom in clear, snappy prose, supported by scores of case studies. *What Exceptional Executives Need to Know* is a must-read for leaders at all levels!"

– LAURA STACK, author, *Doing the Right Things Right: How the Effective Executive Spends Time*

"In *What Exceptional Executives Need to Know*, Elizabeth Jeffries teaches you how to apply her powerful *Executive Mastery Coaching Process*™. With stories and examples from her extensive experience as an executive leadership coach, you'll learn how to bust through communication barriers by speaking the truth in love, holding yourself and your team members accountable, asking on-target questions to get clear outcomes, and much more. This book will refresh you and compel you to practice what you are learning to become a more exceptional leader."

– SETH LANDEFELD, MD, Chair, Department of Medicine, Spencer Chair in Medical Science Leadership, University of Alabama, Birmingham

"*What Exceptional Executives Need to Know* is a must-read for any CEO or leader trying to move their organization to the next level. Elizabeth takes you inside her over 20 successful years of executive coaching and gives real life examples of amazing achievements after goals and expectations are properly set and teams are aligned for success. Her *Executive Mastery Coaching Process*™ can exponentially increase your own effectiveness and quickly help you achieve your full potential."

– TOM KNOX, CEO, SeniorCorp

"Elizabeth Jeffries is the coach's coach and provides advice for executives who want to use the coaching process to strengthen their teams and ignite performance. *What Exceptional Executives Need to Know* is a conversational and accessible book that guides leaders to offer coaching to create top performance. I love the checklists, case studies, and end-of-chapter questions that provide practical tools."

– CATHY FYOCK, Author and Book Coach

"Elizabeth Jeffries is an internationally recognized expert on executive leadership and a celebrated lecturer on human performance. You'll love her latest work on how to coach your team members to get the best of their talent!"

– DR. NIDO R. QUBEIN, President, High Point University

"Elizabeth unpacks the coaching dynamic of *What Exceptional Executives Need to Know* in simple and clear terms. Her approach offers a uniquely different way to coach others to grow and be coachable. She makes it clear that true executive mastery comes when we can grow each team member, and she demonstrates how to do it."

– THOMAS J. WINNINGER, CSP, CPAE, Author, *Thinking Smart*; Founder, Uncommon Companions

"Practical, inspiring and real, *What Exceptional Executives Need to Know* links current business cases with spiritually centered, step-by-step coaching strategies. If you are in the C-suite, or are anywhere near it, this brilliant executive level coaching guide, penned by seasoned, senior-level leadership advisor Elizabeth Jeffries, is a message you can't lead without!"

– MICHAEL ALAN TATE, Author, *Design a Life that Works and The White Shirt*

"Elizabeth Jeffries is the real deal! You will immediately want to put into practice the leadership principles she shares in *What Exceptional Executives Need to Know* that flow out of her extensive experience as an Executive Coach who has helped scores of leaders master their executive leadership effectiveness!"

– BOB TIEDE, Author and Blogger @ LeadingWithQuestions.com
Cru, Global/U.S. Leadership Development Team

"Drawing upon her decades of experience as an Executive Coach, Elizabeth Jeffries has provided us with an engaging and practical book that will assist you in becoming a better leader yourself while you raise the leadership quotient of those around you. This book will help make you a better manager, leader, and coach to your team members."

– BOB RUSSELL, Retired Senior Minister, Southeast Christian Church

"Elizabeth Jeffries is short on cheap advice and long on seasoned wisdom. She is like a trainer who can coach leaders to grow in tangible, practical, measurable ways. Her work as a coach, in seminars, and now in writing *What Exceptional Executives Need to Know*, will put tools in your hands for leading high-performance teams."

– THE REVEREND DR. JOHN P. CHANDLER, Leader of Spence Network,
Author, Speaker, Consultant

"Effective leaders need to master the skill of coaching to lead their teams to unbridled success. Elizabeth Jeffries is a master at this process! Her five steps outlined in her *Executive Mastery Coaching Process*™ provide a systematic framework to address any coaching opportunity for any team member in the organization."

– VAL GOKENBACH, DM, RN, MBA, Vice President/Chief Nursing Officer,
Baylor All Saints Hospital

"*What Exceptional Executives Need to Know* is a leadership book that reads like a story – filled with personal experiences that allow the reader to deeply connect to the coaching concepts Elizabeth shares."

– DR. DEBRA CLARY, Leadership Educator, Speaker, Author, *Executive Women and Leadership*

"*What Exceptional Executives Need to Know* is a clear, concise blueprint on how to be a coach to your team members. Elizabeth has put in writing what she so effectively has practiced during her career as an exceptional and sought-after executive leadership coach. Her book is a refreshing read and an invaluable tool for new and experienced executives."

– JUDY LAMBETH, President/CEO, Maryhurst, Inc.

"Elizabeth Jeffries shares her passion for coaching leaders by inviting the reader on a journey. The result is a rich and practical understanding of how to help others achieve extraordinary results. Using authentic stories, shared insights and analysis, and self-reflection exercises, her process of effective leadership coaching is clear and inspiring!"

– TRACY A. ORTELLI, PhD, RN, CNE, ANEF, Executive Vice President, Postlicensure Nursing

"Elizabeth Jeffries has written a must-read primer for leaders who wish to coach their teams to accomplish extraordinary results that will increase their impact and contribution to the organization. The engaging and relevant case studies drive home the "lessons" throughout and make *What Exceptional Executives Need to Know* a refreshing read."

– CYNTHIA J. BROWN, MD, MSPH, AGSF, Parrish Professor of Medicine and Director, Division of Gerontology, Geriatrics, and Palliative Care, University of Alabama at Birmingham

"Elizabeth Jeffries is a master executive coach! In her latest book, *What Exceptional Executives Need to Know,* she shares how to be the kind of leader who asks the right questions to develop others and create a high performing team! This book will save you years of life experience, cutting your learning curve to become an outstanding leader."

– SHAWN KENT HAYASHI, Author, *Conversations for Creating Star Performers*

"*What Exceptional Executives Need to Know* served as an immediate personal "tune-up" for me. Elizabeth's detailed, commonsense approach to coaching and her powerful *Executive Mastery Coaching Process*™ works!"

– CHRISTINE STESNEY-RIDENOUR, FACHE, President, Beaumont Hospital – Trenton

"Elizabeth Jeffries does a masterful job walking readers through how to enable their team to achieve exceptional outcomes. The structure, examples, and call to action make this mandatory for any executive's library. However, readers who want to get the most from the book will be best served to read it with a highlighter, post-it flags, and a pen to take notes in the margin and immediately apply the lessons."

– DAVE BONNSTETTER, CEO, TTI Success Insights

Dedicated to
William J. McGrane, CPAE

Contents

PART IV: Five Core Skills for Producing Extraordinary Results

Appendices: Deep Dive Into Validated Assessments

A Letter to My Readers

It was a national convention of the American Health Care Association in Washington, D.C. I had just presented a message on sales behavior to over a thousand health care leaders charged with keeping their long-term care facilities full.

After my presentation, an excited, high-energy woman named Dee Ann Campbell introduced herself to me as the senior vice president of marketing with Episcopal Senior Communities, a large continuing-care organization in California. Dee Ann shared her vision for her organization and how she wanted her team to better connect with potential clients. If they could do that, she was confident they could meet their goal of a full census in all five of their communities. She asked if I would come and help her team of sales people better understand their own behavior and that of potential clients and, therefore, become more effective leaders of the sales process.

One conversation led to another, and over the course of our three years together, we put systems in place, census increased, profits rose, people grew professionally and personally, turnover was nonexistent, and I found a new outlet for my passion, talent and skills: coaching leaders to accomplish extraordinary results!

I was and continue to be amazed at the outcomes people can achieve when roles and expectations are clear, goals are set, an accountability process is put in place, and progress is affirmed through celebration. People are so much more capable than they think they are.

Since that first coaching assignment some 20 years ago, I've had the privilege of coaching scores of executives, managers, and leaders in service industries such as health care, banking, associations, churches, and more. Each person showed me what they were capable of, and it was always more than they thought it would be. I simply held up the mirror, asked a lot of questions, and reminded them who they were. It's been a privilege to ask the tough questions, wait for responses, and "speak the truth in love." It's such joy to watch eyes become brighter and smiles spread wider as people say, "Yes, I can do that!" or "Look what I've accomplished!"

All the stories in the following pages are of amazing leaders I've had the privilege of coaching one-on-one over the years. Names and situations have been adjusted for privacy, but their stories are real, their responses to the coaching process are accurate, and most importantly, their fabulous insights, actions, and breakthroughs are true. It has been and continues to be quite a ride!

I've always felt that if I were effectively doing my work as an executive leadership coach, my clients would be able to do with their teams what I had done with them. To make it easier for my clients and for you, my readers, I've compiled my proven *Executive Mastery Coaching Process*™ in this book to help YOU be the coach of your team so you can bring out the very best in each person.

This book is for you, a leader and influencer of others, if:

You already have a good team of people but know that each of them has the capacity to be even more effective, more efficient, and more joyful in their work.

You believe your leaders are already doing a good job

(or else they wouldn't be in their current roles) but wonder whether they could do a GREAT job and feel more fulfillment in their work. What if they discovered they had more talent and gifts than they realized? What would it look like for you and the organization if they tapped deeper into their roles, clarified responsibilities, learned new skills, measured progress, and were ready for even more success?

A team member is about to be promoted, has moved into a new role and needs clarity to master it, or is just stuck and needs renewal. Perhaps you are doing succession planning and need to prepare more people to fill new roles. Perhaps you just selected a top performer, and they need a specific onboarding process. If so, it's time for you to put on your Coach's Crown, learn how to speak the truth in love, and get the very best out of your top talent.

This book will show you how to coach your team members to develop the skills that will increase their impact and contribution to the organization and move them to greatness. I will provide you with a roadmap to get you from the first conversation to the final "Congratulations; well done!" I promise you will be excited and feel renewed to see how your team members are able to break through old thoughts and habits and develop into star performers. And you'll grow right along with them!

This book is also for you if you know you are responsible for teaching, developing, and growing your team but can't invest the time to do it yourself. You still need to understand the principles of coaching and the skills and tools required to achieve great outcomes. Then, as the leader and role model, you can pass this book and coaching process on to your next level of leaders.

Finally, this book is for you if you are a CEO or key senior leader in your organization who wants a coach but understandably can't use someone within the organization. If that's the case, this book will help you better understand a professional coaching process, what to expect, and the questions to ask when you are interviewing an external person.

OK, come on! Let's get started. I'll walk alongside you and be YOUR coach!

Elizabeth

Elizabeth Jeffries
November 2017

Coaching is the fastest,
most powerful way
to develop leaders
at all levels.

– ROBERT HARGROVE

So That's What Coaching Is!

Many words are often used interchangeably but have different meanings. In Part I, I'll clarify what I mean by the word "coaching" and explain the difference between such words as "management" or "leadership." By knowing the root of each word, the meaning will be more clear, and you'll know when to use which word.

*The growth
and development
of people is
the highest calling
of leadership.*

– HARVEY FIRESTONE

The Master Appeared

The first time I saw him, he was in the hallway of the National Speakers Association convention, where I was a fairly new and young member. He was a large man, over six feet tall and large in girth. The environment itself was noisy with hundreds of people rushing through the halls to the next session, laughing and talking, the sound of heels clicking on the marble floor.

What caught my eye was the stillness of the man, the focus and concentration on the one person he was with. His eyes never veered from her face. A few people tried to get his attention, but he was there for her only. The rest of the world didn't exist. I watched him ask her questions and wait patiently while she formed her answers. He never changed his position. He continued to softly look at her. I watched the body language of the woman as she pondered his questions, searched her brain for comments, and replied to him, sometimes showing astonishment and joy at her own answers.

At that moment, I knew magic was happening across the hall, and my soul said, "That's for me! I want to be able to do that!" Then I thought, "No, no, I HAVE to learn to do that!" And for sure I wanted someone to do that for me. I longed for someone to honor me with questions – real questions – and to listen – really listen – to my answers. I knew intuitively that if they asked and listened, I'd break through to places I'd never been before. I knew I'd grow and learn and leap over walls to the new experiences on the other side!

So I waited (it seemed like hours but was no more than 10 minutes) for the conversation to end. Then I quickly walked over to this giant of a man who literally towered over my five feet, put out my hand, and said, "I need to know you. I want you to teach me how to do what you just did in the past 15 minutes in communication with that woman."

So the student was ready, and the master appeared. Bill McGrane taught me the art and skill of asking questions and challenged me (often kicking, screaming, and resisting) to discover, unleash, and break through old thinking and habits to be more and do more than I'd ever dreamed of. He didn't just open new doors to me; he shoved me through them, all the while encouraging me and reminding me of who I was and what I was truly capable of.

Bill was my first coach, long before I knew exactly what a coach truly was. And he's not been my last. I've since had a business coach, a fitness coach, a nutrition coach, a tennis coach, a travel coach, a bridge coach, and a personal development coach, and I currently have a book coach to help keep my feet planted as I write this book!

Each of these people facilitated my learning in their area of expertise. They helped move me from where I was to where I wanted to be. In their own style, they each had a process, a roadmap, a step-by-step plan to ensure I would achieve my goals. They coached, I did the work, I got the results, and we celebrated! And their reward? They experienced the amazing feeling of fulfillment because they shared, they gave, they pushed, they asked, and they may have even heard a voice from on high say, "Well done, good and faithful servant."

YOUR JOURNEY: A Call to Action

1. Name a coach you've had in your life or career and the purpose of that coaching (e.g., fitness, sports, career, etc.)

2. What did that person say or do that caused you to think or act differently?

3. What did that person say or do that you do NOT want to say or do as you coach your team members? (Remember that you also learn by identifying the behavior you see or language you hear that you DON'T want to model.)

4. What outcomes or learning did you experience from your work with that coach?

5. What feedback did you get from others about those outcomes?

6. How did you celebrate your successes?

No person can lead others except by showing them a future. A leader is a merchant of hope.

– NAPOLEON BONAPARTE

Is It Leadership, Management, or Coaching?

These terms seem to be used interchangeably sometimes and can be confusing. Each word, though, has a different meaning and application. Let's take a look at all three.

MANAGEMENT

What gets measured gets managed.
– **William Thompson, Scottish Physicist**

The word "management" comes from the Latin word "manus," which means "hand" and refers to the hands on the reins that hold or lead a horse. The hands control the horse to guide it where the rider wants it to go. Management, then, is a controlling function. It encompasses the tasks and the systems that make an organization run, such as budgets, staffing, tasks, structure, performance indicators, organizational charts, and scheduling. These are continuously repeated, and often the processes are the same each time.

LEADERSHIP

The secret to success is good leadership,
and good leadership is all about making the lives
of your team members or workers better.

– Tony Dungy, Former Head Coach, Indianapolis Colts

The word "leadership" has as its root "to go." It's about
going places, about guiding and influencing others to move.
Influence literally means "to flow from." It's also about what
flows from the leader that causes people to follow. Leadership
is about relationships and people and moving them toward
a clear vision. It's been described as an art because it's based
on a specific form, yet every time it's applied, the outcome
is different.

For instance, my friend Marilyn Swan is a talented artist.
She designs and makes beautiful porcelain jewelry. She has
mastered the art of working the raw porcelain, firing the
pieces in a kiln, painting the delicate earrings and pins, glazing
them, and so on. Yet every time she applies her artistic skills
to the materials, the finished piece is beautifully different.

Thus it is with leadership. Every time a leader interacts
with a team member, the outcome is different because each
person is different. No two conversations are alike because no
two people or relationships are the same.

While most managers are also leaders, you can be a leader
without being in a management position. If you influence
followers, you are living the leadership role. Many executives
have unclear boundaries between these roles. They manage
when they should be leading. They get stuck in the weeds of

the operations instead of creating the vision and ensuring that people see it and live in it. Both managers and leaders need to coach their team members by switching attention from the activity to the person. That's where your role as coach comes in.

COACHING

> *Everyone needs a coach. It doesn't matter whether you're a basketball player, a tennis player, a gymnast, or a bridge player.*
> – Bill Gates, Cofounder, Microsoft

The word "coach" comes from the French word "coche" meaning one who instructs or trains. The word was first applied in education. Students used tutors to prepare for exams. The Oxford University slang for a tutor became "coach" because a tutor carried students to their goal of passing exams.

For leaders in the workplace, this is how I define leadership coaching today:

> **Leadership coaching** *is facilitating an individualized, thought-provoking, creative communication process that moves people to achieve their desired outcomes with commitment, accountability, and enthusiasm.*

While leadership coaching always starts out as work and career related, I've never coached a leader where the process didn't flow into his personal life as well. You can't put each part of yourself in a box. You are a complex being, and who you are at home can't be disconnected from how you show up at work. That's why knowing the person on multiple levels is so important. You can't coach in a vacuum.

You may experience any of the following issues as you coach your leaders in the work environment. Someone may:

- Be dealing with the illness of a family member.
- Be in the process of divorce.
- Have a daughter starting college.
- Have a husband who is in deep depression.
- Be about to get married.
- Have just been diagnosed with breast cancer.
- Be worried about retirement.
- Love their part-time business more than their executive role.
- Have recently inherited a large sum of money.
- Be deeply afraid they can't do the new job.
- Have serious financial problems.

This is just a partial list of what you may experience in coaching leaders. If a team member has any type of personal concern, rest assured that it will come up at some point. You don't have to be a psychologist or have a doctorate in communication to pick up on these issues. Just care, be curious, be observant, ask good questions, and be patient enough to wait for a response. Then you can determine if and how the situation affects their work. Watch for more on developing these skills in later chapters.

The definition above of leadership coaching includes some key words and phrases. Leadership coaching is **thought provoking** because a coach asks questions, probes a bit deeper, waits for a response, and causes the team member to think differently or see something through a new lens.

It's **creative** because responses will often be new, unpredictable, revealing, and accompanied by comments such as "I never thought of that!"

It's all **communication** as you form a common union based on a relationship of trust and respect. It's about connecting with each other, being on mutual ground with clear goals and expectations. It's trusting that the process will lead to joyful surprises and new possibilities.

When coaching consciously and intentionally, it's a process. There's a clear roadmap, a series of action steps taken for the purpose of achieving a specific end result. Watch for the chapters on the full coaching process in Part II.

Coaching is always **about your team member**, the person you are coaching. It's never about you, the coach, and your agenda. It's about their desired outcomes. Sure, a coach offers options and shares ideas and insights from their expertise, experience, and expectations, but all decisions are those of your team member.

Coaches need to be curious, to ask questions – sometimes pretty tough questions – to get the person to see options and potential outcomes, to consider alternate ways to solve a problem, to shift behavior or reframe language. A coach's role is to hold up the mirror and help their team member see themselves with new eyes.

And most importantly, a coach needs to be a truth teller. You have to be willing to "speak the truth in love." You need to be direct, clear, kind, consistent, and brave, challenging your team member to stretch. You can't be afraid to call him on habits such as procrastination, poor time mastery, or judgmental language. You need to help her see herself as others do and ask questions and more questions and then be quiet and still when she's uncomfortable with her own answers.

Commitment! For coaching to be effective, the person being coached needs to have full commitment. She has to be "all in." He's "gotta wanna." If not, coaching just won't work. In the classic book *Think and Grow Rich*, Napoleon Hill lists 13 steps to riches (riches being anything in life you want). The first step, he says, is desire. Hill compares desire to a coin with two sides. One side is definiteness of purpose, and the other side is goals. With these two clear qualities, coaching is on its way to success!

Accountability! Accountability simply means the "ability to account for" what we said we'd do. Watch for much more in Chapter 18 on this important skill and how to help your team members be accountable to themselves, their team, and to you, the coach.

Enthusiasm! What an exciting word! In sales language, to connect with a buyer and make the sale, the last four letters in the word enthusiasm – i, a, s, m – stand for "I Am Sold Myself!" Unless a person is excited about learning and growing and is really sold on the process, is sold on you, and can visualize outcomes, the success potential will drop.

> *Nothing great has ever been*
> *achieved without enthusiasm.*
> – **Ralph Waldo Emerson**

EXECUTIVE MASTERY COACHING

In addition to the full and detailed explanation on coaching shared above, Executive Mastery coaching implies there's an outcome of mastering a process and the skills to get to new outcomes. That's what you want your team member to experience: a sense of "oh my gosh, look what I accomplished!"

Since the goal in a coaching process is to awaken and create new awareness so that the person can literally break through to new thinking and action, you will regularly witness this right in front of you as your team member experiences herself differently through your questions and feedback. That's why asking the right question with integrity and speaking the truth in love are such critical coaching skills. These skills can be learned, and I'll teach you! See more on this topic in Chapters 13 and 15.

IS ALL LEADERSHIP COACHING THE SAME?

There are several ways to view leadership coaching. One is to see it as an opportunity to help people grow and learn new knowledge and skills. Another is to see it as a way to correct a particular attitude or behavior. Here's more detail on these two views of developmental coaching and performance coaching.

Developmental coaching is facilitating the development of a person to reach their next level of attitude, knowledge, and/or skills in their work environment/career. The word "facilitate" means to "make easy," and that's what a coach does. She makes it easy, or at least easier, for her team member to grow in the way they think, what they know, and/or what they know how to do.

At the senior level in an organization, I've found that

developmental coaching is generally the type of coaching that's requested from an internal or external coach. It's often a perk for people with high potential, and it's eagerly sought by people who want to grow in their careers, their lives, and their organizations. When a leader is accepting a new job, part of her signup package often includes a coach to help with onboarding.

CASE IN POINT

A banking organization was experiencing transitions and changes. They were looking at leaders who had potential to step up to new roles. The chief financial officer (CFO) was a master at business finance but would need deeper leadership and relationship skills if he were to be promoted. So we set goals for him, focusing on developing his skills in reading people, communicating "with his whole self" versus just focusing on numbers, and learning how to engage people in more meaningful conversations. With focus and practice, he stepped out of his comfort zone and grew significantly in these skills both at work and with his family. He was soon offered a more senior corporate position.

Developmental coaching usually focuses on creating a higher level of self-awareness, observing how others respond to you, fine-tuning communication skills, and growing in the five competencies of emotional intelligence (or EQ). (See further information and details on EQ in the appendix.)

In addition, some leaders just need a sounding board to talk out situations or options. Developmental coaching helps many leaders to process externally, to hear their own voices, and to discuss situations so that they can get better clarity and take action.

James was an experienced vice president with a critical role in his organization. He had recently been asked by the president to take on an important additional role that was new to the organization.

In my first coaching sessions with James, we worked through the new role, clarifying responsibilities, expected outcomes, timetables, and people. We soon discovered this role was very fluid and needed continuous adjustments based on emerging issues. In subsequent coaching sessions, James found what helped him most was to talk out issues, ideas, and concerns. My role was to listen, ask questions, challenge his ideas, and help him think through these situations. Each coaching session was different and unstructured with emphasis on James' current needs. It was exactly what he needed from a coach at that time.

For aspiring executives, a coach's role often focuses on helping these leaders get out of the weeds and operate in the bigger picture. It's easy to get caught up in day-to-day tasks and forget to look up and out!

Lynn had been promoted a short time ago to a director role. She spent most of the first months putting out fires, building trust, and figuring out where she wanted to lead her team. She replaced a person who had been director for some 30 years and whose leadership and communication styles were quite different from hers. He was minimally involved with a rather laissez-faire style and let the team pretty much do as they may.

In reviewing Lynn's assessment reports, it was clear she was a big-picture thinker. In fact, her scores in that area were well beyond the average. She was a high achiever with a strong sense of urgency. She was also wise and mature enough to know she couldn't rush in and make the needed changes immediately.

Staying true to her gifts, talents, and skills, Lynn crafted a big vision with a strategy on how to get there, the first step being to select an executive leadership team to bridge the gap from being a stagnant department to one of full engagement.

Occasionally Lynn would get in the weeds, get discouraged or angry at the minutia she had to deal with, and then realize once again what stimulated her joy. When she stayed in the vision, relied on her competent executive leaders, delegated appropriately, coached and encouraged her team, held her team accountable, and celebrated successes, she was in her leadership element! This was pure joy to her, and it showed in her body language, her cheerful attitude, and the results the department produced.

Developmental coaching is usually a challenging, fun, and very rewarding experience for both the coach and the team member. When your team member is highly motivated to step out of her comfort zone, stretch to new ways of interacting with people, hone a critical skill, or create new systems to function more efficiently, it's exciting and humbling to be a part of the process. That's when you, as her coach, fall asleep at night with a smile on your face knowing you made a difference in someone's life that day.

Performance coaching is facilitating a process to correct an attitude or behavior that is interfering with performance outcomes. This is a different type of coaching than the focus of this book, and there are many other resources available to help you. Attitudes and behaviors are difficult to change and require a longer coaching commitment. Sometimes performance coaching is a last resort, which makes it even more difficult for everyone.

Many leaders tend to avoid this type of coaching because it's uncomfortable, because they don't want to rock the boat and have conflict, and/or because they lack the skills to speak the truth to others.

Regardless of how challenging performance coaching can be, it's still the role of the leader to address unacceptable attitudes or behaviors as quickly as possible. If you don't address it, you are really saying it's OK. Speaking the truth is the leader's responsibility and is a gift to the person as well as to the team and the organization. Don't wait for unacceptable attitudes and behaviors to escalate to the point that your human resources department has to get involved.

IS EVERYONE COACHABLE?

Some people want to learn and grow. Some people like things just the way they are and have no intention of changing. Others have potential to grow, and that potential can be realized depending on the circumstances. Let's look at stories of each.

CASE IN POINT

The CEO of a hospital that was one of a three-part hospital system called. He told me his key leader, Nancy, had recently been promoted to chief nursing officer and chief operating officer (COO), and he wanted to offer her some coaching to help her adapt and excel in her new role.

In my preliminary conversation with Nancy, I heard excitement and enthusiasm. She was ready to learn and grow, to expand her thinking about this role, and she was eager to have a coach walk alongside her to help her master new skills and learn to think differently and bigger.

Nancy was "all in" from the first conversation through the end of the next year! She worked on visioning what she'd like to see in her nursing department, learned more about herself and her team, and created a plan on how she could expand her impact in the health system overall.

Nancy did all that and more. She was and is the ideal developmental coaching candidate. Watch for the rest of the story on Nancy near the end of the book.

CASE IN POINT

I'd been serving a corporate client for several years, developing their leaders individually and in teams. An executive called one day and asked if I'd work with Susan, one of his company's key leaders. As always, I asked questions such as, "What's going on that makes you want to offer Susan a coaching opportunity?" and "Did she request coaching, or is this your request?"

"Well," he said, "She doesn't seem very happy. Her work is OK, but she's lagging behind in some things. I'm not sure what's going on. I haven't talked with her about coaching, but I'd like to offer it to her. I'd like to keep her if she wants to stay here."

The executive shared a bit more information along these lines and with my request that Susan call me for discussion, he promised to talk with her that day. (Having a potential coaching client call me versus me calling them allows me to evaluate her initiative and learn how interested she really is in doing her part in a coaching process).

Several days later, Susan called my office. That was the first clue: It took several days before she reached out to me. In 15 minutes of conversation it was obvious Susan wasn't a good candidate for coaching. She complained about the company, her boss, her team, and the work she was doing. She was clear she didn't want coaching with anyone. I encouraged her to be candid with her boss about her issues and check out other approaches for help. She was not a good candidate for coaching because she simply didn't have the "I wanna."

CASE IN POINT

A prominent medical center had recently hired a new COO. From the get-go, there were challenges. Nurses complained about his lack of compassion, he came across as rude and brusque to everyone, and he was critical, pushing his ideas rather than engaging others about their needs or explaining why changes needed to be made.

Could I help? As always, I asked questions and more questions to get a clearer picture of the situation. I learned that the new COO had come from a strong leadership position in manufacturing. He was aggressive, loud, and pushy. He didn't understand the culture of a medical center or the passion of the nurses and other staff to care for patients. While he was an extraordinary strategist with a proven history of success, he hadn't yet been able to adapt to a very different culture.

In our conversation, he treated me the same way as he treated his coworkers. He was not willing to even consider flexing his style, much less to learn how to do that. He was not a good coaching candidate at that time.

This one is not solved yet! His competency is high. His relationships skills are low. Maybe he'll be more open to coaching in the future. His pain just isn't great enough yet.

People don't change until the pain of the present is greater than the pain of the change.
    – Tony Robbins, Life Success Coach

YOUR JOURNEY: A Call to Action

On a personal level, how coachable are YOU? How willing are you to grow as a leader? How willing are you to learn coaching skills that will help further develop your team members?

_____

_____

_____

_____

_____

_____

_____

_____

_____

_____

_____

_____

_____

_____

_____

_____

_____

_____

_____

_____

_____

_____

_____

_____

_____

*You cannot teach
a person anything.
You can only help
him discover it
within himself.*

– GALILEO GALILEI

The Leader's Role as Coach

What about you? You've probably had coaches in your life and career. Do you think of yourself as a coach to your team members? Have you thought about the potential outcomes for them, for you, and for the organization if you, on purpose, designed a coaching plan with each of them? I don't mean just a quick, one-on-one, monthly meeting where you discuss progress, she leaves the room, and you don't have much connection until next time. I mean getting to know each person on a personal level, their dreams and fears, their goals, their passions, their competencies, their gaps. I mean sharing a vision, setting expectations, planning, challenging, asking the tough questions, waiting while he thinks out the answers, cherishing the amazing outcomes, and so much more.

You, as a leader, have expertise and experience. If you have the "I want to," you have the power to change the trajectory of the lives and careers of each of your team members and enrich your own in the process.

Are you willing to give up what you know and explore what each of you doesn't yet know? Are you willing to be a truth teller, holding up the mirror to help a person see themselves through a new lens?

CASE IN POINT

Alice is a competent and experienced director of her division of a large organization. She was having difficulty with Mary, a team member who wanted to leave her current role and start a new and larger role within the department.

While the idea had some merit, Alice felt Mary wasn't experienced enough to take this on. She had only been in her current role for a short time, had minimal leadership experience, and wasn't particularly liked and respected by the rest of the team that she would have to lead. Alice wanted to keep Mary in the department because she had good potential, but she had to figure out a way to discourage her in going after this new role now while still keeping her engaged and happy.

Alice decided to gently explain the above perspective to Mary, to be a truth teller, to speak the truth in love to her and offer a six-month coaching opportunity. Alice explained that she would coach Mary herself, and together they would identify what the new job would require in behavior and skills and would then create a plan to work toward those goals. While this wasn't exactly what Mary wanted, she grew appreciative of the personal coaching opportunity. She was able to see a larger scope of the new job and areas she hadn't considered.

Through her leadership coaching, Alice was able to keep a valued team member and help Mary grow into a top contributor in the department. Mary saw she wasn't quite ready for the new role and worked diligently on her own development to prepare for a bigger role in the future.

WHAT DO YOU BELIEVE ABOUT COACHING?

People look at me and see a calm, cool guy
on the sidelines, and I want them to know
that my Christian faith affects my
coaching and everything I do.

– Tony Dungy, Former Head Coach, Indianapolis Colts

As a leadership coach, you can't hide who you are. Your attitude about people, about life, about work, and about coaching will show, and it will be instrumental in how successful the coaching process is for the team member, for you, and for the organization.

Take a few minutes and think about what you believe about people and about coaching. Ponder the statements below and indicate with a yes or no whether you believe the statement or not.

I BELIEVE:

Effective leaders are made, not born. Skills can be learned. Layered learning over a period of time is more lasting.

People are capable of breaking through old thinking and habits. They may not know it yet.

Coaching is critical to performance excellence.

It is a privilege to be someone's coach.

The coaching relationship is a sacred one.

People provide the primary commitment and enthusiasm to achieve their stated outcomes. Coaches facilitate and augment the process, holding the person accountable for their commitments.

The role of the coach is to comfort the disturbed and to disturb the comfortable.

A coach asks more of people than they would ask of themselves.

Not coaching is a disservice to the development of a team member.

Not coaching a top performer is a financial loss to the organization.

A coach's role is to speak the truth in love.

A coach believes that what you permit, you promote. If you allow unacceptable behavior, you are saying it's OK.

YOUR JOURNEY: A Call to Action

Hopefully you noted YES to all 12 of the above statements. What additional thoughts and beliefs do you hold about coaching and your leadership role as coach?

_____

_____

_____

_____

_____

THE EXECUTIVE MASTERY COACHING MINDSET

OK, so you know a lot about many things. You have many years of experience and a deep skill base. You've been successful in your career and in your organization.

Caution! Yellow flag! Oops! You don't know everything,

so be careful thinking you do. When you think you have all the answers, you have a serious case of what my colleague Keith Webb calls know-it-all-ism. The illness, he says, causes those afflicted with it to be blinded to opinions, answers, and solutions other than their own.

Coaching is never about you. It's always about the person you are privileged to coach. You are the one who asks the questions, the one who helps your team members discover their own answers. If you want to have a tough, ineffective job as a coach to your team members, just tell them what to do, have an answer for everything, interrupt their comments and questions, and wear a smug expression to assure them you're smarter than they are.

If, however, you have a mindset of mastering skills and have the heart of a servant, if you ask good questions, listen in, wait for a response, and humbly share insights, you will truly make a difference in the life and career of your team member.

DEBUNKING COACHING MYTHS

Honesty is the first chapter in the book of wisdom.
- Thomas Jefferson

There are many beliefs about coaching, and many are false beliefs that cause people to shun the idea of engaging a coach because they don't truly understand the purpose and positive outcomes of professional coaching. Here are a few myths that may come up in conversations about leadership coaching with your team members.

Myth: Successful people don't need a coach.
Truth: Professionals have coaches. Amateurs don't. Think of tennis star Roger Federer and basketball star LeBron James.

Myth: People who get feedback all the time don't need to be coached.
Truth: You don't know what you don't know. Leadership coaching is about creating new possibilities and growing as a person.

Myth: Executive leadership coaching is the same as counseling or psychotherapy.
Truth: Executive leadership coaching focuses on workplace behaviors, actions, and results related to your job and career goals.

Myth: Executive leadership coaching is only to fix last-ditch efforts.
Truth: If a situation reaches this point, coaching is needed more. Prevent last-ditch efforts by doing ongoing developmental coaching.

Myth: Executive leadership coaching can't be measured.
Truth: Look at what can be measurable: increased profits, higher customer satisfaction scores, increased retention, and reduced turnover.

Myth: Executive leadership coaching is just a way of telling people what to do.
Truth: Executive coaching focuses on results using questions to help people discover what they want or need to do.

Myth: I can coach myself or talk to my best friend.
Truth: Neither you nor your best friend will ask the unbiased tough questions that need to be asked and cannot bring an outside perspective.

Hopefully, these truths will help you and those in your sphere of influence more fully appreciate the value of coaching.

WHY COACH YOUR TEAM MEMBERS?

What are your reasons to be a coach to your team members? What's in it for you? What's going on in your organization that makes you think coaching is needed? Review the list below and check all that apply to you.

I have a great team, and I want to see them grow.

I've had help from others in my career, and I want to pass it on.

It's part of our culture to develop leaders.

We've been mandated to more formally coach our team members.

I don't know if I'm a good coach, but I want to learn how to be one.

We are doing succession planning, and I want to prepare people to move into new roles.

Our onboarding process hasn't been too great. I want to make sure our leaders start out well and stay with us a long time.

I've had a leadership coach myself and had a great growth experience.

NEW ROLE, NEW PERSON

Unfulfilled expectations are one of the biggest challenges in communication. You may have a picture of what is expected, but have you clarified it with solid feedback? Too often, we assume. That's why in coaching or consulting, especially when a role is new, we start with what the job requires, or a job benchmark. The story below gives you an example of the questions to ask and how to think about a job to get role clarity.

CASE IN POINT

Cindy had been a leader in a large academic medical center for several years. She had a record of achievement, was highly thought of, and was interested in moving forward in the organization. Since the vice chair for research's role was expanding and she was taking on more responsibility, the chair of the department decided to add a new position of assistant vice chair. Cindy was asked to take on that role, which she enthusiastically accepted.

Cindy was very excited about the new role and moved into it quickly. She had many ideas, but she had no set guidelines or clear expectations for the new role. She was told to get with the vice chair for input and then create a job description based on what she thought was needed.

Cindy was offered an opportunity to have an executive leadership coach and jumped on the offer. When I met Cindy, I was impressed with her positive attitude and her interest in learning more about herself and growing into this new executive role.

Cindy completed the battery of validated assessments and an electronic 360-degree survey, and together we went over the results. Tending to be more of a soft-spoken introvert, Cindy was more comfortable working in the background, avoiding conflict, and just doing her work really well. Her Social Skills competency in the emotional intelligence report showed an opportunity for growth.

Passionate about learning and serving, Cindy also said she was most comfortable with a good structure to guide her work. Among her highest core skills were personal accountability, appreciating others, and goal orientation. Using this information, along with insights from the initial interview, we began a focused discussion on setting three to five goals for her to accomplish over the next six months.

You may already be seeing from the above comments that the intersection of Cindy's needs and her unstructured, undefined new role was going to be the first issue on the agenda. She needed role clarity. Without it, she'd wander and wonder and soon would get discouraged and maybe even be sorry she accepted this position.

Cindy felt she wanted to accomplish the following goals in the months ahead:

Clearly define the new role of assistant vice chair.

1. Determine the three to five Key Accountabilities for this role. What outcomes is this role responsible for producing?

2. Rank each in order of importance and assign a percentage of overall time for each of the Key Accountabilities.

3. Build personal power and presence.

4. "Own this role:" Project confidence and the power the role innately holds and speak with authority.

5. Build new relationships and strengthen others.

6. We prioritized these three goals and immediately started working on role clarity, soon addressing how to accept and display her personal presence and create ways to reach out to build new relationships crucial to her new role.

Here are a few of Cindy's comments from her three-month summary about what she was learning and her outcomes so far:

- "Stretching myself to create new relationships and participate in new conversations has been a challenge and fun. I've made a point to meet with someone new to me every month. The goal has been to create new relationships, expand my network, and get to know people on a more personal level."

- "I've also made a concerted effort to literally sit in the front row of many meetings and speak up in meetings."

- "Coaching has given my position visibility and myself in this position, which has increased my self-confidence."

- "Clarifying my role and responsibilities and prioritizing the responsibilities and effort dedicated to each has allowed me to make decisions in this new role."

- "This has probably been the most critical for me. It has helped me communicate my role and responsibilities across the organization. It also has been extremely helpful in determining priority of issues and developing a plan to accomplish my goals and the goals of the position."

YOUR EXPERIENCES AS A COACH

List two people and/or teams you've coached in the past. Did you coach someone to develop a new skill? What outcomes were produced?

Person/Team 1:

How you coached them:

Outcomes:

Person/Team 2:

How you coached them:

Outcomes:

What, specifically, did you learn as you coached in these situations? What did you do well? What would you have done differently? What can you apply from those experiences to coaching your next team member?

*The formulation
of the problem
is often more
essential than
its solution.*

– ALBERT EINSTEIN

PART II

The Executive Mastery Coaching Process™

This section takes you through a five-step process of how to coach a team member, what to say, what tools to use, and how to evaluate success. It's your roadmap to get you to the outcomes you want.

LET'S MAKE A PIE!
Not exactly that kind of pie, but close! Just add a few letters before "pie," and you're really close. Read on!

It's not only
what we do,
but also what
we do not do,
for which we
are accountable.

– MOLIERE, FRENCH PLAYRIGHT

The Five Steps in the *Executive Mastery Coaching Process*™

There are five steps in the *Executive Mastery Coaching Process*™, and they are easy to remember if you use the acronym ADPIE.

1. Assess
2. Diagnose
3. Plan
4. Implement
5. Evaluate

Let's use a simple example to illustrate this pie. Say you're running late for work because you stopped at Starbucks for coffee and quickly filled your new insulated thermos and popped it in your purse. At work, you get to your desk, grab your phone from your purse, and try to turn it on – but it won't start! Now what?

1. **Assessment.** First, I'm going to ask myself why it isn't turning on. Then I notice my phone is wet and everything in my purse is wet too!

2. **Diagnosis.** Hmmm. It seems my coffee leaked out of my thermos onto my phone. So my phone probably won't turn on because it's soaked with coffee.

3. **Planning.** Uh oh, I really need my phone today. I decide I need to call one of the great fixer-uppers in IT, knowing they'll come to my rescue.

4. **Implementation.** Now I have to do something, take action. This is where I run across the hall to John in IT who can fix anything electronic.

5. **Evaluation.** This is the final step where John tells me, "Joan, we saved your phone, and it works fine. Next time, it would be best to make sure the cap is secure on your thermos!"

WOULD YOU LIKE TO BE COACHED, SAM?

It's time now to think about a high-potential person on your team. You're ready to bring up the idea of coaching to help this person discover more of who he is and his capacity for taking on new roles and responsibilities in the organization. Consider the following situation.

You have noticed that Sam has been doing a great job in his current role as a manager in your organization. His work has been on time, on target, and on budget. He contributes good ideas in management meetings, he has a positive, can-do attitude, he gets along well with people, and he seems to like to try new things. You wonder if there's more that Sam can contribute and if he's open to growing to new responsibilities, especially because you don't want to lose him. You decide to have a conversation with Sam and approach him.

"Sam, I've been thinking of setting up a defined coaching plan to help you grow," you say. "Have you ever had a coach? Would you be interested in some one-on-one work like this?"

Sam responds, "Oh, did I do something wrong? Is that why I need coaching?"

Don't be surprised if you get a similar response from a team member at first. If developmental coaching is new to your organization, Sam may not see the purpose of this yet. Some people still think coaching is to correct something they've done wrong and don't yet see it as an opportunity to explore new goals and career advancement. Remember the coaching myths in Chapter 2?

Now you can explain to Sam that he's actually done some things very right and that you want to help him grow his knowledge and skills, so he can possibly take on new roles and responsibilities.

You explain that his work has been very good. He's a good thinker. He makes things happen and gets excellent results in his department. He's well liked by his team and other department leaders too. You believe he may have more talent than he's been using. Now Sam is interested!

Next, you explain the coaching process to Sam, so he knows what to expect. Follow the ideas and process as described in the following chapters, so Sam has a clear picture of what he's signing up for as well as his responsibilities.

Across the next five chapters, we'll look at each of these five steps and how we can adapt them to our coaching process, so you can coach Sam and other team members into their success zone.

I am always wary of decisions made hastily. This is usually the wrong thing. I have to wait and assess, looking deep into myself, taking the necessary time.

– POPE FRANCIS

Assessment

Assessment is a vital part of the coaching process. It forms a foundation to better understand Sam's strengths, opportunities for growth, knowledge, skills, interests, passions, and personal and career goals. Assessment is accomplished in several ways, including the interview and using validated assessments and surveys.

THE INTERVIEW: GETTING TO KNOW HIM

Start with interviewing Sam to learn more of his personal history. Make this a conversation versus constant questions, so he won't feel he's being interrogated. This builds rapport and shows that your interest in him extends beyond work. It builds trust, which is the basis for a relationship. Inevitably you will find connections you didn't realize you had, such as similar backgrounds, faith or church connections, parallel interests and talents, people you both know, etc. (We're assuming you already know marital status, children, and some of Sam's obvious preferences.)

Here are sample questions you can start with. Assume that each response may elicit another question not listed here. While you are interviewing and processing Sam's response, you will begin to formulate ideas that would be helpful for him to address. Asking Sam's permission to take notes on those ideas during the interview shows respect. The amount of time involved for the first interview is approximately 30 minutes to one hour.

- Where are you from originally? (This tells you more about the culture he came from and could be instrumental in him accepting a promotion that involves travel or relocation. It's also a check on your own personal, unconscious biases.)
- Tell me the parts of your current job that you love?
- Tell me the parts of your job where you are so "in the flow" that you lose track of time?
- Which parts of your current job cause time to drag when you do them?
- How would you define your current talents? What are you really good at?
- Is there a role in the organization that would excite you and spark your passion and creativity?
- What additional knowledge do you feel would better prepare you for your next role in the organization?
- What new skills would you like to learn that would be an advantage in your next role here?
- What current skills need to be tweaked or honed? These are things you are good at but would like to do better.
- What feedback have you received about your behavior and how you interact with others?
- What feedback have you received about your knowledge base and what you are good at?
- What feedback have you received about the level of your skills?

- What have you been affirmed for in the past?
- What's working for you now in your job?
- Are you stuck anywhere? If so, where?
- What, if anything, needs to change? How come? What would it look like if it changed?
- What questions do you have for me? Is there anything you'd like to know about me?

USING VALIDATED ASSESSMENTS AND SURVEYS

Validated assessments are one of the most powerful tools in the coaching process. I can't imagine coaching without them! Assessments hold up the mirror for people to see themselves through an objective lens. They open communication, create awareness, and are used to help develop coaching goals.

From the coach's perspective, assessment reports share deeper information than you'd likely get in an interview only; they also provide information that prompts further questions when you meet.

Many organizations use only one assessment, often the DISC model or the Myers-Briggs model, measuring only behavior or type. However, I highly recommend using a battery of assessments to get a better picture of the person that will help you jointly develop a pertinent plan of action.

Using the medical model as an example, let's say you feel nauseated and have pain in your abdomen, so you decide to see your physician. She will no doubt do more than just take your temperature. She'll likely ask questions, take your blood pressure, run several lab tests, and perhaps order other tests, so she can diagnose more accurately.

Good coaches use multiple assessments for the same

reason. You can't tell enough about a person with just one assessment. There are many excellent assessments in the market today. I use and can highly recommend the following five validated assessments that measure behavior, driving forces, core competencies, acumen, and emotional intelligence. I'm trained and certified through Target Training International/TTI Success Insights and have used these assessments with thousands of clients. They are validated, reliable, and easy to administer and interpret. TTI is a researcher and developer of the following instruments:

- **Behavior** – how a person behaves and their ability to interact with and respond to others.
- **Driving Forces** – the why or the drivers behind people's actions and passions.
- **Core Competencies** – the level of development and ranking of a leader's 25 core skills and the connection to what their job requires.
- **Acumen** – understanding and applying eagerness and depth of discernment for problem solving and decision-making.
- **Emotional intelligence** – the five hierarchical competencies that build strong relationships and high levels of collaboration required in leadership – Self-Awareness, Self-Regulation, Motivation, Empathy, and Social Skills.

Note that the appendix includes details on this battery of validated assessments, including how to order them and/or be trained and certified for your own coaching processes.

These assessments are available online, and the person you will coach experiences them while you go on with the 360-degree assessment.

The amount of time involved for Sam to experience the online assessments is approximately 45 minutes.

360-DEGREE ASSESSMENT

One of the best ways to help a team member grow, develop, and become more productive is to allow that person to see themselves through the eyes of others. This can be done in one of two ways: a verbal or electronic 360 survey.

A VERBAL 360 SURVEY

- Together, you and Sam choose five to six people who know him well and have worked with him for a minimum of six months. They should include a combination of his peers, direct manager, and direct reports.
- Sam notifies each person to be interviewed and explains that he is excited to be starting a professional one-on-one leadership coaching process and has given their name to share insights with you.
- You (or an independent person/consultant) meet with or phone and interview the people you and Sam selected. Assure each person that the information is anonymous and will be used to help Sam develop and grow.
- Ask each person a series of questions, such as those listed here. Each response will most likely initiate another question from the interviewer.
  - How long have you known/worked with Sam?
  - What is Sam doing well?

- What do you see as his talents and gifts?
- How do you observe how others respond to him?
- How does he contribute to the culture of his department/organization?
- What do you see as opportunities for growth for Sam?
- If you were coaching Sam, what main area of his behavior and skills would you suggest he focus on for continued growth?

The amount of recommended time involved to interview each person is approximately 20 to 30 minutes. Combine the information from these interviews into two separate documents: what's working well for Sam and what are Sam's opportunities for growth.

ELECTRONIC SURVEY

- Choose a 360 survey developed and tabulated by a reputable outside firm that will guide you through the entire process.

- As in the verbal 360 process noted above, together you and Sam choose five to six people who know and have worked with him for at least six months. This should be a combination of his peers, direct manager, and direct reports.

- A letter goes out to each person from a key leader to whom Sam reports, explaining that they've been selected to participate in a survey that is designed to gather information for Sam's personal and professional growth. Participants are given directions to respond online and are assured that the survey is anonymous and that there is no way to identify individual people or their answers.

- A report is tabulated electronically and returned to you.

The amount of time involved for each respondent to complete the 360 survey is approximately 20 minutes. The information from the 360 survey, whether verbal or electronic, plus the results of the assessment reports is shared with Sam in the second meeting and is used to guide the goal-setting process.

The amount of coach's total time involved in the assessment phase is approximately six to 12 hours. Most of your hands-on work as a coach is up front in this phase. The time to conduct personal interviews is three to four hours if not doing an electronic 360 survey, plus three to four hours to conduct the personal interview with Sam, debrief all reports, and along with Sam, set three to five goals to be addressed and accomplished over the next six months.

*Bedside manners
are no substitute
for the right diagnosis.*

– ALFRED A. SLOAN, FORMER CHAIRMAN AND CEO,
GENERAL MOTORS CORPORATION

Diagnosis

Y ou've gathered some foundational information to better understand Sam, his personal history, his experiences, his preferred behavior, his passions, the ranking of his core competencies, the way he sees the world and himself in the world, and his level of emotional intelligence. You've received feedback from several people in his sphere of influence at work. You're building a deeper relationship and trust, and you see good potential and some possibilities for suggested target goals.

A CONVERSATION WITH YOURSELF

Now it's time to step back and ask yourself some questions. Take all the information you've gathered, analyze it for patterns, and list a few educated guesses as to what would help Sam, and identify potential goals. Following this roadmap is an integral part of "making a diagnosis." Possible questions to ask yourself:

- How ready is Sam for coaching? Use a scale of 1 to 10, with 1 being "not ready at all right now" and 10 being "he's ready; let's schedule our next meeting."
- What's his level of motivation to grow through coaching? Again, evaluate on a 1 to 10 scale.

- How coachable is Sam? Is he willing to give up being the one who knows or the one who's right?
- How solid are his listening skills? Does he listen and ponder an answer or does he wait to talk?
- How clear is he on his career interests?
- Does there seem to be anything blocking him from moving forward?
- Is there any conflict, either real or imagined?
- What is Sam's preferred style of communication?
- What behavior do I need to flex in my style to connect with him?
- How likely is Sam to break through to new thinking and actions?

Once you ask yourself these questions, you'll have some initial thoughts as to what would be of help to Sam. Write down your thoughts, observations, and possible goals. Writing them down will help with the next step of talking with Sam and, together, setting goals.

EVALUATING POSSIBLE GOALS FOR SAM

As a result of all the gathered information, you may be thinking all sorts of things, like:

1. Sam says he has trouble saying no. He takes on a lot and could get stressed out if he keeps doing that. Looks like learning to ask questions before saying yes or no would be helpful. Delegation strategies and skills also would be important for Sam's growth.

2. Sam's style shows he has some challenges with managing his time. I'll check to see what systems he's using, how he

plans his work, and if he procrastinates. Working on time mastery will be a good goal to explore.

3. Sam seems to avoid conflict. He's a peacemaker; while that's good and valuable in any job, perhaps some help in understanding conflict is good. Learning and practicing skills to manage conflict would help.

4. I've noticed in Sam's EQ report that his Self-Awareness and Self-Regulation are a little low. There are some practice exercises in the report that will help him with this, which could lead to significant breakthroughs for him.

5. I see on Sam's Driving Forces report that he's motivated to lead and be in charge. He's also motivated to learn and is curious. I'll explore that a little more too and figure out how to capitalize on those talents.

6. Sam scored pretty well in the Core Skills Ranking. He's all about people, and it shows here too. Decision-making is a critical skill as a top leader. Sam's score shows he's just moderately developed in this skill. I'm going to put this on the list for a possible goal to work on.

YOUR JOURNEY: A Call to Action

What other thoughts would you have about Sam, his probable issues, and potential goals?

_____

_____

_____

_____

_____

Men often oppose a thing merely because they have had no agency in planning it or because it may have been planned by those whom they dislike.

– ALEXANDER HAMILTON, A FOUNDING FATHER OF THE UNITED STATES

Planning with SMART goals

After thinking through all the information from the 360 survey and the assessment results, you've most likely formed some ideas about a probable "diagnosis" and what might be helpful for Sam.

Now it's time to plan the SMART goals with Sam. He's got to be totally engaged in setting the goals and see the reasons for them and the potential positive outcomes. So it's back to more questions to help Sam think about what's in it for him. Prepare some questions such as:

- How's your interest in better managing your time, Sam?
- How would it help you if you had a more effective system? What outcomes do you see that producing?

This is where the three- to four-hour meeting occurs with Sam that's mentioned at the end of Chapter 3, where you debrief all his leadership assessment reports and feedback from his 360 survey. Together you will talk through ideas and jointly agree on three to five goals to accomplish over the next six months. SMART goals are defined below, along with an example.

SMART goals are specific. They are focused and clear with each goal addressing one issue. Being specific sparks the motivation to achieve the goal. The statement "I will be a better listener" is too general, but "I will practice active listening with one person each day and record outcomes" is very specific.

SMART goals are measurable. Having goals you can measure helps you track progress, stay motivated, and feel the excitement of getting closer. The statement "our goal is to reduce turnover by the end of the year" is not measurable, but it becomes measurable when you say, "We will reduce turnover by 10 percent by December 31."

SMART goals are attainable. Goals need to be realistic and attainable. They need to make you stretch but still be possible. Be aware of setting goals that you don't have power over. A goal of achieving a promotion in three months doesn't work if promoting you is someone else's decision. Stating "I will learn all the skills to be head of human resources in three months" is probably not realistic. However, the goal "I will learn all issues about compensation in three months, which will bring me closer to HR certification" becomes attainable.

SMART goals are realistic. The goals you set need to matter to you and need to be in alignment with other goals in your life. Sample questions to ask yourself: Is it worthwhile? Is it the right time? Do I have time for the training to achieve this goal?

Consider the statement "I will earn a master's degree by the end of two years." You might want a master's degree, and you know it will probably help advance your career, but can you realistically devote the time to it right now with two small children and responsibilities at home? Is it worth the sacrifice of time right now? If not, consider this: "In preparation for committing to another degree, I will research master's programs at five universities and compile and compare information, completing this by August 1."

SMART goals are timely. Every goal needs a timeframe, so you have a deadline to focus on and work toward. Otherwise, other tasks will slip in, and the goal will keep moving forward with little results. Take "as soon as possible" out of your vocabulary! Note that all the examples stated above are time focused.

CASE IN POINT

Following are goals for Lisa, a competent and caring health care executive I worked with some time ago. This is a six-month process designed with and agreed upon by Lisa.

Core Strengths from Lisa's verbal 360 Survey

- Clinical excellence.
- Leadership and communication skills.
- Highly respected by all.
- Passionate about her work.
- Caring, kind, and fair.

Core Strengths from Lisa's Personal Talent Skills Inventory

- Personal relationships.
- Attitude toward others.
- Sensitivity to others.
- Empathetic outlook.
- Theoretical problem solving.

Developmental Opportunities for Growth

- Work and personal life balance.
- Delegation.
- Self-confidence and assertiveness.
- Team communication.

Lisa's SMART goals

The primary goal for Lisa is to build a healthier and more balanced lifestyle so that she is rejuvenated and more productive as a leader and has higher self-confidence and assertiveness. The goals are written in the first person so they are personal and meaningful to Lisa.

GOAL 1: Create a healthier balance between work and personal life.

Actions include but are not limited to:

- Journaling daily to become more self-aware of my work patterns such as phone calls at night and weekends and length of my workday.
- Keeping a time log for two weeks to increase my awareness of work habits.
- Establishing boundaries and clearly communicating these to others when appropriate.
- Scheduling time for personal pursuits such as physical exercise, family time, and hobbies.

Goal 2: Develop stronger delegation skills.

Actions include but are not limited to:

- Journaling daily to become more aware of how work is taken on and distributed to my team.
- Identifying tasks and projects suitable for delegation and to whom.
- Working with regional and district team members to coach them on how best to execute the tasks that I've delegated to them.

GOAL 3: Project higher self-confidence and assertiveness with others.

Actions include but are not limited to:

- Journaling daily to increase awareness of what/when situations trigger emotions, lesser self-confidence, and passive behavior.
- Breathing consciously to center myself and gain composure when emotions begin to rise.
- Exploring yoga classes for centering and pacing.

GOAL 4: Develop more effective communication with my team.

Actions include but are not limited to:

- Discussing work/personal boundaries with team members to facilitate better time mastery for all the team.
- Meeting with each team member to determine their needs/ preferences regarding how much communication they need from me and when.
- Scheduling time with each team member individually based on their needs.

Success in these goals would be demonstrated by:

- Receiving positive feedback from my direct leader and other team members that I seem more relaxed and less stressed.
- Feeling and expressing more self-confidence and assertiveness, clarity in roles, and deeper communication with my team.
- Receiving positive feedback from my team members that their communication needs are being met.
- Journal notes that I've left the office by 5:30 at least three times per week.

YOUR JOURNEY: A Call to Action

List three ideas and/or insights from this goal-setting activity that will help you be a more effective coach. From these larger goals, we'll now move into the implementation stage, where weekly commitments will be made and acted upon.

_____

_____

_____

_____

_____

_____

_____

_____

_____

_____

_____

_____

_____

_____

_____

_____

_____

_____

_____

_____

_____

_____

_____

_____

_____

Implementation: Just Do It!

At Walmart, if you couldn't explain an idea or concept in simple terms on one page, Sam Walton considered the idea too complicated to implement.

– Michael Bergdahl, **Former Director of People, Walmart**

I mplementation is simply taking action and carrying out the plans on the goals that have been set. These are the short-term goals, worked on in one or two weeks, with specific actions that lead to accomplishment of the larger goal.

This is where your team member schedules meetings with you, reads assignments, practices skills, journals outcomes, documents responses from people, asks questions, and gets specific feedback.

Remember that people process information differently; some will take action quickly, while others will need thinking and processing time. Consider this when working on implementation/action. Ask questions such as:

- What would you like to accomplish until we meet next time in two weeks/one month?
- When do you think you can complete that goal?
- Is there anything that will block you from completing this?
- Would you agree to journaling a few notes daily about your

observations of yourself and how others respond to you? Implementation can be done in different ways:

- From each of the three to five goals, take one action weekly or biweekly, make a commitment, and just do it!
- Review all the goals from a helicopter perspective. Decide which of the goals is most important to you and will bring the greatest rewards or outcomes the quickest. Choose that one goal, focus on a specific action from that goal, and just do it!

IMPLEMENTATION TECHNIQUES

Responsibilities of the Coach/Leader. As the coach, you'll need to do some preparation for your meetings with your team member. Following are areas to check on to ensure you're ready, that you've followed through on any promises you've made and cleared your space, so you can avoid distractions while together.

1. Prepare by reviewing notes from the last session.
2. Make sure you did what you said you would do. Did you promise to send an article or a book or agree to make a connection with someone for your team member? If you didn't do it, why not?
3. Be available at the appointed time and remove all distractions so you can focus on the person.

Responsibilities of the Person Being Coached. The following information is set up in a way that will help you explain verbally or present in writing the responsibilities of your team member in the coaching process. Share with your team member.

1. You'll experience an online, comprehensive, validated battery

of leadership assessments that describe your preferred leadership and communication style, your workplace motivators/passions, your level of emotional intelligence, your acumen or the way you make decisions, and 25 ranked core competencies. These assessments will help you know yourself better and help you set meaningful goals.

2. While you are taking the assessments, a series of four to six perceptual interviews or an electronic 360 survey will be conducted to discover how others perceive your leadership, communication style, and overall effectiveness. Together we'll decide who in your sphere of influence will participate. This may include a board member, your immediate leader, several peers, and/or direct reports. An optional spouse feedback interview by phone or in writing is also available if interested. (I love adding a spouse interview to the process. A spouse is a truth teller and can be an advocate for the process. This is only done with permission of your team member).

3. The first meeting is three to four hours where I will debrief the information from the interviews and assessments. Together we'll create a customized development plan that clearly defines your goals and expected outcomes.

4. Subsequent meetings will be held onsite or by phone every two to three weeks for a period of six months. Each meeting or phone conversation will be scheduled for 60 to 75 minutes. Sessions are set to layer learning and practice new skills and/or behaviors. We'll meet in (give the name of the meeting room) or if we meet by phone, please plan to initiate the call at the appointed time. We'll schedule the next meeting/call at the end of each session.

5. At the end of three and six months, you'll be responsible for writing a learning summary based on the initial goals. I'll send you a one-page document with questions to complete.

6. Recording and journaling goals and actions are part of the coaching process. Please select a journal or notebook to record insights, observations, actions, and outcomes to discuss when we meet.

7. Please choose an accountability partner from within the company to walk along with you during the coaching process. Plan to connect with this person once a week for support and encouragement. (A full explanation of internal accountability partnerships is included in Chapter 18.)

8. Please schedule two hours of quiet reflection time every week during the coaching process. This is generally your thinking time. Use it to reflect on decisions that need to be made, ideas and plans you want to explore, or new projects you want to outline. Find a quiet place, preferably first thing in the morning. Consider working from home, a coffee shop or a conference room, but someplace where you won't be disturbed.

CASE IN POINT

A question on the three-month coaching summary is "how has your coaching experience, to date, already caused you to grow as a leader?"

In response, Jason, one of my executive coaching clients, wrote this: "I think the most important thing I have learned is that I have to be intentional about change. I am now taking a half day per week to work offsite, and it has helped me greatly in keeping up and planning for the future. I also have realized that it is OK to admit that I can't do everything and I need help.

"Additionally, journaling has been a new rewarding experience for me. It has greatly increased my level of self-awareness. It forces me to think about both what went well in a given day and what I could have done differently."

DIALOGUE FOR A 60- TO 75-MINUTE COACHING CALL OR MEETING

The following is a template you can follow each time you meet with your team member, either personally or by phone. You are in the role of Susan.

Susan: "Hi, Sam. It's good to see you today. Come on in."
Sam: "Thanks, Susan. It's good to be here."

Because you know Sam likes to warm up a bit before plunging into work conversation, you ask how his vacation plans are coming along, or refer to whatever you know is going on in his life personally. You both chat a few minutes rather than delve immediately into work conversation.

Susan: "OK, Sam, you know we start our time together with questions and always start with the same one! Has anything come up for you since our last meeting that we haven't yet discussed?"

Sam may want to discuss something new that hasn't been on an agenda before. This is very likely to happen since you haven't met for two to three weeks. If so, just explore it.

Following are additional questions and comments that are routine and can be adapted for each session. These are just the starting questions; others will follow depending on Sam's response. Start with questions relating to the action steps set at the last meeting:

- Sam, I promised to send you that article on executive presence. I did, and you received it, right? What was meaningful for you from the article?
- What ideas or discoveries have you applied since we last talked?
- Tell me a story from your journal connected to the goals you set last time.
  - What worked well?
  - What could you have done differently?
- Sam, you told me that Janice is your internal accountability partner. How did your meeting with her go?
- What did you reflect on in your quiet time these past two weeks?
- What action steps would you like to take between now and our next meeting that will move you closer to your big goals? (Sam sets several action steps, and you both note what was promised. You'll start your discussion next time by checking with Sam on how he managed the action steps and the outcomes, as above.)
- Last question, Sam. Same as always. Specifically, what was one thing from our discussion today that was especially meaningful for you?

This is a great question for the end of the session. Sam goes away anchored to something meaningful, and Susan learns more about Sam, what was important to him, and what types of issues to focus on in the future.

On the emotional side, Sam feels good because he had an awakening, an "aha" moment, or made a specific decision on something important. Susan feels great because she connected with Sam on something meaningful to him.

SHALL WE END OR CLOSE?

Too often we simply stop at the end of a coaching conversation – or a meeting, for that matter. Nothing is anchored; there are no specifics as to what happens next or who's responsible for what. We tend to let ideas hang and just simply stop and move on to something else. Consider these two ways to complete the session:

1. OK, Sam, that's about it for today. I'll see you at our next appointment in a few weeks.

2. Sam, you've done some great work these past two weeks. Thank you for your full engagement in this process. You are a joy to work with. I look forward to talking again in two weeks as planned.

By "closing" versus "ending," there's a sense of completion.

YOUR JOURNEY: A Call to Action

At your next conversation or meeting, check yourself on whether you are "ending" or "closing."

_____

_____

_____

_____

_____

Every night before
I go to sleep, I analyze
every detail of what
I did that day. I evaluate
things and people, which
helps me avoid mistakes.

– **COMPAY SEGUNDO, CUBAN MUSICIAN AND COMPOSER**

Evaluating Your Coaching Success

You're a professional and want to do this process well and help Sam break through to new outcomes. This is the part where you determine if and how you've been successful in coaching Sam. Evaluate yourself after each meeting and at the end of the entire coaching process.

After the session is completed, simply ask yourself these two very familiar questions that you expect Sam to ask himself:

- What worked well today? (This helps you celebrate it and repeat it when appropriate.)
- What could I have done differently to help Sam? (Note what you learned that you would not do again or do in a different way.)

THE EXECUTIVE MASTERY COACHING CHECKLIST

Here's a checklist to more specifically evaluate your own coaching at the end of a session or the end of the process. Rate yourself on a scale of 1 to 10, with 1 being "not too great" and 10 being "very well done."

I listened attentively and didn't overly interrupt.

I managed my silence and waited for my team member to respond.

I offered the opening question "Has anything new happened since our last discussion that's not on our agenda that you'd like to discuss?"

I remembered to flex my style to better communicate in the style of my team member.

I asked pertinent questions to elicit thinking and good decision-making from my team member.

(If appropriate) I recognized my positional power and worked on relating from a coach perspective vs. a boss perspective.

I affirmed my team member on the progress she's made.

I offered insight and advice when appropriate.

My body language projected interest and engagement in the process.

My tone of voice demonstrated caring and support.

I kept the meeting to the allotted time.

I closed the meeting by debriefing the session and setting a date for our next meeting.

YOUR JOURNEY: A Call to Action

What would it take to be a 10? Consider a situation where you coach someone with this ADPIE coaching process:

1. Assessment. How did you gather information? What tools and resources did you use? What information did you accumulate?

2. Diagnosis. With the assessment information, what was your educated guess about this person and their probable needs?

3. Planning. What questions did you ask? What agreements did you come to with the person you are coaching? How many goals? When would they be accomplished? Who is their accountability partner?

4. Implementation. What tools did you offer to help the person accomplish their goals? Will you document? How often will you meet?

5. Evaluation. What changes did you note in the person or the process? Did you get feedback from others? What measurements worked? How did you affirm and encourage your team member?

How did you evaluate your own coaching and your growth? On a scale of 1 to 10, how competent are you in each of the five steps?

SCORE:

#1 _____   #2 _____   #3 _____   #4 _____   #5 _____

If you are not a 10 now in ADPIE, what would it take to be a 10?

*Let me adjust
my crown and
get my day started.*

– FROM THE WRITINGS OF MAYA ANGELOU

PART III

The Coach's Crown:

The Five C's of Communicating in the Coaching Process

This section explores and explains the five necessary elements to incorporate in your coaching process. They include what it means and what it looks like to believe, live, and act with care, clarity, and connection, plus how to convey support and get commitment from the person you are coaching. When you apply all five of these elements, you are, indeed, wearing your "Coach's Crown."

*Seek opportunities
to show you care.
The smallest gestures
often make the
biggest difference.*

– JOHN WOODEN, FORMER HEAD BASKETBALL COACH, UCLA

Demonstrate Care

THE LEADER BECOMES THE SERVANT

One of the blessings that comes with experience and longevity in the world of work is a gradual change in perspective. By the time you become a senior leader, usually there is a shift in your focus from self to others. You have little to prove to yourself anymore. Confidence is high, but you have a sense of humility, not arrogance.

Richard Rohr in his book *Falling Upward* says of this time, "Life is more spacious now, the boundaries of the container have been enlarged by the constant addition of new experiences and new relationships. At this stage, I no longer have to prove that I … am best. I am not preoccupied with collecting more goods and services; quite simply, my desire and effort – every day – is to pay back, to give back to the world a bit of what I've received."

So you begin to see your role more now as a coach and mentor versus one of just "getting things done." You are evolving more into the role of trusted advisor, an advocate, and a true servant leader.

PRINCIPLES OF SERVANT LEADERSHIP

Following are fundamental truths and motivating forces

upon which servant leadership is based. They are in total alignment with the principles of masterful coaching.

- Servant leadership is a spiritual concept – meaning the non-physical, the higher self, the divine, the soul of a person. The leader wants to bring out the best in followers, and the best is always linked to their spirit.

- A servant leader is a beacon of light and clearly and courageously articulates the vision of the way things could be. They go out ahead to show the way because they more clearly see where it is best to go.

- Servant leadership is based on humility. Ego and power needs get in the way of service. Leadership and management expert Dr. Ken Blanchard refers to ego as "Edging God Out."

- We have to be authentic with ourselves to be in relationships with others. Only then can relationships be healthy and flourish.

- The true natural servant understands through listening in and being present to the moment.

- To serve others, we have to nurture and develop ourselves. We can't give away what we don't have.

- The process of transformation to the way of a servant leader starts inside the person, not in others, the organization, or the world.

- There is no path TO servant leadership, only a path OF servant leadership.

We are spiritual beings having a human experience.
– Pierre Teilhard de Chardin, *The Phenomenon of Man*

The concept of servant leadership was brought to light in the late 1960s by Robert Greenleaf, a retired executive with AT&T. A humble Quaker, Greenleaf believed that a leader is first a servant. He outlined a philosophy and a set of practices for the purpose of enriching the lives of individuals, building better organizations, and ultimately creating a better and more caring world. Servant leadership is both a leadership philosophy and a set of leadership practices.

Working with the Greenleaf Center for Servant Leadership (now the Spears Center for Servant Leadership) some years ago, I taught others about Greenleaf's 10 characteristics of a servant leader as identified by Larry Spears from Greenleaf's work. A conference was held each year, and leaders from health care and other industries gathered to understand what it means to be a servant leader and how to develop the characteristics.

The concepts and characteristics are simple, yet not always easy to follow. That's why there is no road TO servant leadership, but only a road OF servant leadership. There are, however, some signs that can be noted in one who is on that path.

TEN CHARACTERISTICS OF A SERVANT LEADER

The servant leader is a servant first…. It begins with the natural feeling that one wants to serve, to serve first. Then conscious choice brings one to aspire to lead. That person is sharply different from one who is a leader first, perhaps because of the need to assuage an unusual power drive or to acquire material possessions …. The leader-first and servant-first are two extreme types.

– Robert K. Greenleaf

1. **Active listening** means to understand the other side and to listen completely before making a decision. It's asking questions for clarity and listening to understand the response of others.
2. **Empathy** requires paying attention and putting yourself in the other person's shoes. It's listening without judgment.
3. **Healing** in the context of servant leadership is to help make whole those with whom we come in contact, to ease conflicts in relationships, and build community.
4. Servant leaders have a strong **awareness** of what's going on around them.
5. Servant leaders exhibit **persuasion**, meaning to build consensus through influence and persuasion rather than taking advantage of positional power.
6. Servant leaders exhibit **conceptualization**, thinking beyond day-to-day realities to long-term goals.
7. Servant leaders have **foresight**, the ability to foresee the likely outcome of a situation by connecting the past and the present.
8. **Stewardship** entails a commitment to serving the needs of others, the organization, and its mission for the greater good of society.
9. **Commitment to the growth of people** is seen in appreciation and encouragement of others and their growth.
10. **Building community** refers to showing appreciation and praise for others' contribution through making relationships work.

For further resources and study on Greenleaf's work on servant leadership, contact Larry Spears at www.spearscenter.org.

Several centuries before Greenleaf wrote his missive on

servant leadership, another man taught us about the beliefs and behaviors of a servant. The apostle Luke, in the Gospel according to Luke, quotes Jesus of Nazareth: "Let the greatest among you become as the youngest, and leader as one who serves" (Luke 22:26, NIV). In essence, servant leadership is about service over self and needs to be the attitude of anyone who coaches another person. Servant leadership sparks the question: "Whose feet can I wash today?"

So a leader/coach needs to have the heart of a servant, caring for and caring about the people entrusted to his care. Here are a few questions to check yourself and see how adept you are in demonstrating care as a servant leader:

- Are you genuinely interested in others' growth and building leaders?
- Do you have self-confidence enough to allow someone to grow beyond you?
- Can you step back and allow the person to shine?
- Can you move your ego out of the way?
- Do you come from a position of love, compassion, and reverence for people?

CASE IN POINT

Seth Landefeld, MD, is chair of the Department of Medicine at the University of Alabama in Birmingham, Alabama. I first met him when I was brought in by Jean Ann Larson, PhD, leadership development officer, to solidify our plan to develop his team of vice chairs and division directors. It was clear from our first conversation that Seth already had a great team of physician leaders. He simply wanted to help them grow and become even better personally and professionally.

After many questions about the team and expected outcomes, we set dates for a two-day teaming session along with the full battery of assessments and 360 surveys to be conducted before then. Seth fully participated in the entire learning process himself, responding to all the executive assessments and opening himself to feedback from the 360 survey.

(You may think it's strange to point out that Seth fully participated in the entire learning process, but I've had a few leaders set up a teaming session for their team that they themselves didn't attend. On one session, held at a beautiful golf resort, the CEO introduced me to his team and said he had to leave for a meeting. What he forgot to note was that our room had huge windows overlooking the golf course; when we looked out, we saw him tee off on the first hole. Oops!)

One of the most impressive moments of my relationship with Seth was at the end of the retreat. In his closing comments, he offered the entire team of 22 people the opportunity to continue learning through one-on-one coaching with me for the next six months. Not surprisingly, Seth was the first one to sign up, and he has been an ideal coaching client from the beginning, setting goals, shaping the culture, implementing plans, and fully participating in every meeting or phone appointment.

Seth not only cares deeply about his team, but also cares about his role as a leader, continuously seeking ways he himself can grow and learn. In his humanness, he's not perfect, but he's a perfect servant leader for his team. And they think so, too.

Of the 10 characteristics of a servant leader, which one is your strongest? Which one of the 10 characteristics could use some attention? Here they are again.

    1. Active Listening.

    2. Empathy.

    3. Healing.

    4. Awareness.

    5. Persuasion.

    6. Conceptualization.

    7. Foresight.

    8. Stewardship.

    9. Commitment to the growth of people.

    10. Building community.

ROBERT GREENLEAF'S SERVANT LEADER TEST

Do those served grow as persons? Do they, while being served, become healthier, wiser, freer, more autonomous, more likely themselves to become servants?

– Robert K. Greenleaf

Definiteness of purpose is the starting point of all achievement.

– W. CLEMENT STONE, BUSINESS MAN AND PHILANTHROPIST

Have Clarity of Purpose

A purpose is the reason something is done or why something exists. This applies to you, the coach, and the person you are coaching. It's rather like a mission, which is the "why" we do something.

Let's take a look at both sides of this coin.

Often people assume a purpose is clear and that it's understood what a person who is being coached really wants from the experience. Too often people speak in generalities, without confirming a conversation or without being clear about expected outcomes and why we want them.

Your team member needs to be able to clearly articulate what she expects to have accomplished at the end of the coaching experience and why. Sometimes she may need help articulating her purpose. She just knows she wants to grow but doesn't have specifics. This is where you'll ask questions, including some related to information in her assessment reports and 360-survey results.

KEY QUESTIONS TO LEAD YOUR
TEAM MEMBER TO CLARITY OF PURPOSE

- *What's your purpose for participating in a coaching relationship?*

I want to be a better leader.

- *What, specifically, do you think would make you a better leader?*

Being a better communicator.

- *If you develop that (skill/attitude/knowledge), what would that do for you?*

I'd have a better relationship with my team.

- *What's the ultimate end point of having a better relationship with your team?*

It would show I can do relationships well and give me a better chance to be considered for a more senior role. (Now there's the PURPOSE and it's CLEAR: to be promoted to a more senior role.)

As a developmental coach it's important to know what your team member intends to get from the coaching experience. Otherwise, how will you know the questions to ask or the practice sessions to craft? How can you help her be accountable if you don't have clarity on what her intentions are? Some thoughts to explore:

- Is this process to prepare the person for a new role?
- Is it to build visibility and credibility in the organization?
- Is it to help her see a blind spot?

Examine your own purpose for being engaged in a coaching experience. Is your intention to prevent someone from making the mistakes you made along the way? Do you want to serve and help someone else just because it's the right thing to do? Or perhaps someone helped you or coached you some years ago, and you experienced the value of it and want to give back.

Julie is a senior leader who was promoted to her current executive role about a year ago. As a woman, she dealt with a lot of negative biases along the way, including lower pay than her male counterparts. She felt she wasn't noticed for her hard work, even though she published articles, took on volunteer roles in her industry, and earned additional degrees.

Julie is an advocate for women and is always excited about coaching women in her area of responsibility, so they avoid the experience she went through. That's her clear purpose. She does it in a positive, action-based way where she asks tough questions and speaks the truth in love.

YOUR JOURNEY: A Call to Action

Define your clear purpose for engaging in a coaching relationship with a team member.

The single biggest problem in communication is the illusion that it has taken place.

– GEORGE BERNARD SHAW, IRISH PLAYWRIGHT

Make a Connection

To connect means to show a relationship between one person or thing and another. In the world of people and coaching, it's also about HOW we connect verbally and non-verbally to master deeper and more meaningful communication.

This chapter on connection has several parts because it's really about that huge word COMMUNICATION, which has many parts. It's about forming a common union with another person, a process that involves many factors, including:

- **Content** – the words we speak or write.
- **Context** – when the words are expressed; the timing of our communication.
- **Command** – how words are said or the way we look when we say them.

There are 10 barriers to effective communication, 10 reasons why communication is so tough and complex. Making your communication work is a lifelong learning process. The more awareness you have, the better results you'll experience when you communicate.

BARRIERS THAT KEEP US FROM COMMUNICATING EFFECTIVELY

- Communication is a risky process. We attempt to express and expose feelings without being rejected. There's a limited trust level.
- We talk too much and listen too little.
- We fail to understand the meaning or intent of the message. Our biases and prejudices interfere.
- We pay little attention to nonverbal indicators transmitted by others.
- We interrupt others before they finish what they are going to say. We think we know what they will say, so we step on their words.
- We drift away; we take mental vacations and lose focus.
- We downplay a person's feelings and assume they're irrelevant or no big deal.
- We give advice without being asked and attempt to solve problems with pat answers.
- We ask questions with a hidden agenda of disapproval such as, "You're not going to do it like that, are you?"
- We switch the issue and don't respond to the other person's concern because we either don't know what to say or didn't really pay attention to their concern.

Perhaps one or more of these barriers to communication spoke to you. If so, what would you like to do about it, if anything?

The following ideas and techniques are for you as a coach, but they're also for you to share with the team member you are coaching. Since communication is two way, both of you will benefit from understanding and using these ideas and techniques.

RELATIONSHIPS: THE BOTTOM LINE

In business, relationships really are the bottom line. People buy from people they know and people they like. It seems easy to say, "Well, then, make yourself likeable," but that's easier said than done.

We all buy and sell all the time. Got a new idea you want to get approval for? You need to sell it to the board or your immediate leader. You want to apply for that new executive position? You've got to sell yourself. Want your son to clean his room? You've got to sell him on the idea.

Think about the people in your life whom you connect with easily. What is it about them that makes that connection feel so natural? Here's a short list of statements that people have shared with me:

- They show interest in me by asking questions about my life or work.
- They actively listen when we're in conversation.
- I feel valued when I'm with them.
- Their body language matches their words. They smile. They focus their eyes on me and don't visually wander around the room to see who might be more important.
- They are fully present, not checking email, texting, or reading something while I talk.
- They respond honestly to my questions.
- They are not afraid to speak the truth to me or call me on my failings.
- They return phone calls and emails.
- They ask my opinion.
- They accept that I'm different than them, and they don't try to change me.

- They make me feel important. I'm not invisible to them.

What can you add to this list? What other behaviors have you experienced that make you feel you've connected with the person? All of these statements connect to how you build a relationship with the person you are coaching.

Relationship-building is easy for some people and very difficult and stressful for others. Some people have an internal need for relationships and avidly seek them out. Others have minimal internal needs for relationships and shy away from them or only connect when necessary.

As a coach, you'll need to make a good connection with the Sams and Sallys on your team. Perhaps you'll want to keep the list of the 11 statements above to help remind you about ways you can connect with others. Here are also a few questions for you to ponder:

- How would you approach and connect with a person who is a quiet introvert?
- How would you approach and connect with a person who is more verbal and extroverted?
- How deep is your knowledge of the art, science, and complexity of communication?
- How willing are you to master the art of processing a person during coaching to get to their core criteria, including asking power questions, using focused listening to build trust, giving feedback that can be heard, and reading subtle signals and natural styles of people?
- How are you at allowing moments of quiet and managing silence?
- How would you rate your level of curiosity?

How would you coach the person in the story below? What would you add? What would you do differently?

Jeff is an executive responsible for a large department in a global organization. As a result of my working with the full department team, Jeff asked if he could engage in a coaching relationship with me.

At first glance, you'd read Jeff as a quiet, kind, caring, competent, and experienced leader. He's an excellent listener but somewhat uncomfortable around other people. He seemed to deflect from himself and defer to me or others in conversation. He's a definite introvert, doesn't need the spotlight, and leads more from a collaborative model.

I reviewed Jeff's assessment reports before we met officially. His low score in Social Skills on his emotional intelligence report revealed a gap. However, his Self-Awareness score was in alignment with the norm. This combination told me that Jeff probably knew he had challenges with communicating with people and was interested in doing something about it.

Jeff admitted that he likes people but has a very hard time engaging in conversation with them. His purpose for coaching was to more intentionally build relationships and become more comfortable in social and business situations. Intentionality was his coaching word; he needed to build relationships on purpose in every interaction throughout his day. And this was definitely out of his comfort zone.

Together Jeff and I created specific goals and a plan. Starting small and working with specific questions, Jeff is gradually learning to reach out to people and initiate conversation. He is learning to expand on a conversation versus just responding with short comments. He stops and talks to people in the hallway and asks easy questions. Jeff has been diligent in practicing social skills. He made a list of people whom he didn't know well and consciously made appointments to meet them over coffee, ask them questions, and offer help from his department.

Social skills may never come easy or naturally to Jeff. As a deep introvert, he knows he has to practice regularly, anchor them by journaling his successes, and celebrate his progress. As a result of his work, Jeff has since built genuine relationships and has received positive feedback from his colleagues. He says that makes the work all worthwhile.

PROJECTING A POSITIVE VISUAL PRESENCE

Projecting a positive presence applies to both you when you are coaching and to your team member when he is being coached. Everyone and everything communicates something! First impressions are made with each encounter with a person, not only the first time you meet. Be attentive to:

- **Facial expressions.** Make them warm, including a soft nonjudgmental smile.
- **Posture.** Be erect and face the person you are talking to, which indicates you are paying attention.
- **Body movement and gestures.** Periodically leaning forward into the conversation indicates active listening.
- **Distractions.** Be aware that distractions can kill connection. Put the smartphone aside.
- **Space.** Avoid a barrier between you that cuts off communication. Instead, sit at a right angle or around a corner from each other, which opens communication.

Sitting side by side indicates collaboration and is best used when working on a project together.

- **Handshake.** It seems no one really teaches us how to shake hands, something that definitely projects an image of power or weakness. A firm handshake, coupled with eye contact, is the way to go.

NONVERBAL COMMUNICATION CLUES

Following are some nonverbal examples that will help you read body language of people while communicating. When you talk with someone, you get and reveal meaning not only from your words but also from the way you tilt your head, position your body, move your arms and legs, and arrange your face. Check out the following body language and what each implies:

Body language	What it implies
Arms folded	Closed or defensive/Convince me
Tilted head	Curiosity
Brisk walk, erect posture	Confidence
Spontaneous arm movements	Openness
Raised eyebrows	Disbelief
Hands on hips	Readiness
Swinging foot	Impatience/boredom
Hands clasped behind back	Authority
Hand rubbing	Expectation
Chin stroking	Evaluating
Open hands	Sincerity
Leaning back with both hands supporting head	Superiority

Jack was CEO of a large international nonprofit organization. I was referred to him by another client, so I had not yet met him. He originally called me for help with Kathy, one of his team members. They had some disconnects in communication, and he wanted to help her communicate better.

Recognizing that communication is two way, I needed to meet with Jack first and then with Kathy, which I did. Jack was a very tall, thin, lanky man who literally charged into the room and moved right into my personal space to shake hands. His facial expression was stern and serious. He was obviously a take-charge person who commanded and owned whatever room he was in.

I had yet to meet Kathy, but my first impression was that Jack, with his strong, serious commanding presence, could easily be intimidating to others.

He shared his concerns about Kathy, and I went on to meet with her.

Kathy presented herself as a warm, soft-spoken, gentle yet strong woman. She explained that Jack was not the easiest person to work for. He jumped in with solutions before he heard the whole problem, he was harsh with team members, and people didn't feel listened to or respected. It was difficult to communicate with him, and he tended to blame the team members versus looking in the mirror at himself.

Circling back to Jack, both his and Kathy's issues were now clearer. Jack was a very busy, high-profile executive with huge responsibilities. He hired good people on his team, he said, and he assumed they would all just do their jobs and let him do his.

"I'm not their babysitter," he said. "I've got a lot of work and a lot of stress getting it done."

Since a coach's job is to speak the truth in love, I knew I had to talk with Jack in a way that he'd hear me and see his part in the communication gap with Kathy and probably other team members too. Because his serious, severe facial expressions were so visible and prominent, that was where I began. I was convinced Jack had no idea how he came across to others or how intimidating his facial expressions could be to others. Awareness precedes change, so raising Jack's awareness of his facial expressions and body language became job one.

A fun story had just been reported in our local newspaper, and I happened to ask Jack about it. We chatted about it for a few minutes. Jack relaxed and had a good laugh with a big smile on his face.

I was shocked at the difference his laugh and smile made in his demeanor! He became a likable guy that I wanted to connect with. Aha! There was the door opener. Jack rarely smiled, and most people rarely saw this side of him. As we discussed this, I took out my phone and asked him to position himself as he normally would be, and then to simply smile softly. We reviewed the two photos, and he noticed the difference immediately. He never intended to come across so severe, he said, and he never thought a smile could make such a difference.

Together we created a plan to help Jack soften his facial expressions and body language, beginning with a simple smile. While this didn't solve the full communication issue, it was a great start!

PROJECTING A POSITIVE VOCAL PRESENCE

Vocal presence includes tone of voice, pitch, speed, and volume. The tone of your voice sets the tone of the conversations. Tone is a particular quality, or way of sounding, which expresses meaning or feeling. A voice can sound loving, sarcastic, judgmental, joyful, mean, accusatory, affirming, and so forth. You already know the effect when you use certain tones to get a child to clean his room!

Other vocal presence indicators are speed and volume. These also can affect how a person connects with you. Too fast or loud, and you may be hard to follow. Too slow and soft, and you could lose the person.

Practice saying the following statements in various ways, putting emphasis on different words, and see how the meaning changes.

1. I understand your wish to take Monday off, Sam. It will not be possible.

2. I regret I can't be of further assistance.

3. Congratulations on your award!

4. I understand how necessary this project is, Nancy, and I won't be able to have it finished for you today. (Using "and" instead of "but" makes people remember the first part of the sentence).

5. Since my paper was given to you Monday, why was it completed last?

6. That was not my mistake.

7. You did a great job, Susan. Thank you!

PROJECTING A POSITIVE VERBAL PRESENCE

Language creates feelings and feelings spark behavior.
– Elizabeth Jeffries

Verbal presence refers to the words you use when you communicate. People often don't realize the words they use when they speak and how they can affect our feelings and therefore our behavior. Our brains don't know fact from fiction. When you say things such as, "I can't," it's like your brain says, "OK, you can't, and I'll make sure you can't." When you tell yourself, "I'm having a really hard time with …," your brain says, "OK, I'll make it hard for you."

CASE IN POINT

Margaret was a vice president who had been promoted fairly recently. She was still in a learning curve, and when we began our coaching time, she would start out by saying, "I'm struggling with …." When she used the word "struggle," she actually sounded like she was struggling. It sounded like she was having a tough time with that issue, and most likely she was.

Reframing, she gradually dropped the word "struggle" and substituted "I'd like some help with … " or "I have yet to figure out how to …." Reframing makes a huge difference to the feelings and behavior that follow.

A powerful word to use when reframing is the word "yet." It implies that you are in process of learning something and haven't quite mastered it YET!

Watch and listen for the words you use as well as the words your team member uses. Remember to speak the truth in love to her and ask her to reframe her language, so she's a problem solver and not mired in the problem.

Another aspect of verbal presence is to **manage silence**. This is a challenge for most of us as we have an unfounded tendency to fill the silence in some way. Learning to manage silence is a hugely important skill for a person in a coaching role! Ask a question, wait for a response.

A technique is to ask a question and count to 21 silently. You probably won't get to 21, but it's a target to keep you quiet while the other person forms their response. This is especially important when asking a question of a person who is more of a quiet introvert and needs thinking and processing time to respond.

Using terminology people can understand also affects our connection with others. Most industries and organizations have abbreviations for projects, credentials, departments, tasks, and more. Make sure you understand these abbreviations and ask if you don't.

VERBAL POWER ROBBERS

Following are ways we minimize ourselves by certain statements we make. These statements or questions rob you of your power, diminish the perception others have of you, can make other people uncomfortable, and can lessen your own self-confidence.

Hedging means saying qualifying phrases that are in contrast to definite opinions; when you hedge, you're announcing there will be something wrong. Examples:

- "I may not be as knowledgeable as you ..."
This statement is usually followed by "but" and sets it up so that people don't hear the rest of what you have to say or contribute.
- "I probably shouldn't say anything ..."
If you don't think you should say anything, then don't.
- "The solution may be ..." when you know what it is).
Use a definitive statement when you know what the answer is. Discard "may be" and use "is."
- "Of course, it's only my opinion."
You minimize yourself and your opinion. Leave out "it's only."
- "Kind of," "I guess," and "I tend to"
  These are weak responses. Be clear and definitive and sure.

Tag questions: These are when you add on phrases like "don't you agree?" to your questions. The tilted head with this question shows you aren't sure. If you are sure, say it with clear language, strength, and good eye contact.

The word "try": Erase it from your vocabulary! It conveys lack of confidence and commitment. As Yoda said, "Do or do not. There is no try."

Extensive apologies: An apology is appropriate when you have control over the situation. "I'm sorry it's not better weather" indicates you have the power to control the weather. Consider using the phrase "I regret" when you don't have control over the situation.

Self-effacing remarks, such as "I'm just" and "I'm only": Placing yourself in a lower position with these words isn't humility. It's negating your role or competence.

Asking too many questions: Trailing together too many questions can project weakness.

Justification: The need to explain your actions to others is a power robber when an explanation isn't necessary. Do you need to explain to someone why you won't be able to accept a role on the committee? Can you just say, "Thank you for asking. I regret it won't work for me right now"?

PEOPLE READING

Your skill and ability to read people will greatly affect how the conversation and connection with a person proceeds. When you can read the probable feelings and body language of a person, you can adapt your communication style to her and craft your message and your language to ensure you are indeed connecting.

You don't have to be a psychiatrist, psychologist, or FBI investigator to learn to read people. You just need to know the signals and watch for and pay attention to the subtle signals a person sends.

Reading people enables you to see past just what they say, to know who they are and what they are not saying but feeling. To read people you also need to surrender any preconceptions, biases, or old resentments that keep you from seeing a person clearly.

CASE IN POINT

Attending a learning seminar many years ago with Bill McGrane, at the McGrane Institute in Cincinnati, I was taught the importance of connecting with people and how to do it through **people reading**. Then I was given an assignment to practice this art.

The story below takes you through the process of how

to help people reach their "core criteria." It's the concept of using questions to move people to a place of recognizing and solving a situation, committing to an action, and then being accountable for doing it. It's about getting to the basic or real issue, known or unknown, that's causing unrest in the person.

I've shared the steps of the people reading process below and highlighted key questions and skills.

Bill took us to Izzy's, an informal lunch restaurant in Cincinnati where people just sat anywhere, including at a table with someone they didn't know. My assignment was to sit with a stranger, begin a conversation, and "read" the person with the skills I was learning. This meant I was to physically read their body language, assess their feelings, and engage in a conversation.

The outcome was to connect with a person, lead them through a discussion of some issue in their life, ask the questions so that they would see and solve the issue and commit to take action, and then give feedback. Admittedly, I was scared to death! What should I say? What if they didn't want to talk with me? What if they DID want to talk with me?

This experience was so powerful I still remember it today, some 25 years later, and I'm eager to share it with you.

I picked up my lunch, faked bravery, and sat down at a table across from a man who was probably in his mid-40s. He was dressed casually and had apparently just sat down as his lunch was barely touched. He didn't have any reading material with him, and when I sat down, he smiled politely, then put his head down and avoided eye contact, the signal that he probably didn't want to talk. But my assignment was to get him to talk! "OK, here goes," I thought. Here's how the conversation went.

"Is it OK if I sit here?" I asked cheerfully.

"Sure," he said.

"Isn't it a beautiful spring day? It gives me lots of energy. Does it do that for you?" I asked, choosing language that would create an opening for a safe dialog.

"I guess. But not today," he mumbled, head down.

"Oh, gosh, it sounds like something took away your sunshine today," I said, showing I was listening.

He sat silently, eyes diverted, head down, shoulders slumped. I **waited** for his reply. ("Wait," my coach had said. "Even when it's a long pause, don't fill the gap.")

Eventually, he said, "Oh, I had words with my wife before I left home this morning, and the conversation is still going around in my head."

I was shocked at the time at how quickly a total stranger made such a personal statement. However, since this encounter, I've flown over two million miles, and frequently the stranger seated next to me on the plane will tell me their story after I begin people reading.

"That can sure take away internal sunshine. It sounds like you didn't leave each other in a very good space this morning," I said, waiting for a comment and then waiting some more.

"That's for sure, and I've been distracted all morning," he replied.

"Hmmm, do you have a plan to do something about this?" I asked, giving him an opportunity to reflect on what I'd noticed when I asked the question.

"Not really. I guess it will solve itself," he said.

"Does that usually work for you all? Letting it solve itself?" I asked.

"Not really. But we ignore it, and somehow we just go on," he replied sadly.

"I was taught something by a very wise person who helped me one time. I'd be happy to share it. **Are you open to hearing a suggestion?**" I asked.

"OK, I guess," he replied.

"He told me when I avoid a situation, it just makes it worse," I said. "Resentment builds and can accumulate and cause more issues. He told me that if I have a conflict and don't talk it out, I'll act it out. In other words, those feelings of anger or remorse or whatever they are will come out sideways and cause more problems. Do you think that's true?"

There was a long pause.

"Oh, is that ever true," he said sadly with his head down.

"So believing that, **what would you like to do, if anything,** about the conflict with your wife from this morning?" I asked slowly.

"I guess I'd better fix it," he said.

"**What would it look like if you fixed it?**" I asked quietly.

"Well, I could call her and apologize because I see now I was wrong," he said with a bit more energy.

"**Is that something you want to do?**" I asked with a calm voice.

"Yes, I want to do that. I hate when we fight," he said, straightening his posture in the chair.

"**When** would you call her?" I asked softly.

"I could call her as soon as I finish lunch," he replied.

"**So are you saying that's what you will do?** Call her after lunch?" I asked to confirm what I heard him say.

"Yes, I will definitely call her and apologize. She's everything to me, and I want to fix this," he said.

Remember that I didn't know this man. He didn't know me. This conversation had taken no more than 10 minutes. I was new at people reading. I knew there's one more step, and I was in the flow, so what the heck, I would just ask it.

"**How would I know you've called her and dealt with the conflict?**" I asked.

"Well, I could let you know," he said.

"I'd love that. **How will you let me know?**" I asked.

"I'll send you a note," he said excitedly. (This was when email was rare and texting was nonexistent.)

"**When can I expect the note?**" I asked.

"No later than next Friday," he said.

We finally exchanged names and then exchanged contact information, shook hands, and said our goodbyes.

His name was Matt. As promised, he sent me a note about a week later. Seems he did indeed call his wife and initiated a conversation where he apologized, and they repaired the conflict from the morning.

Matt shared in his long note to me that apparently he always had a hard time apologizing and did it rarely. His wife was so amazed that he took the initiative to heal the conflict that it brought them to a new level of love and intimacy.

PROCESSING PEOPLE TO REACH THEIR CORE CRITERIA

The above story took you through the process of how to help people reach their "core criteria." It still amazes me how safely framed questions, listening in, and giving feedback can move people to a place of recognizing and solving a situation, committing to an action, and then being accountable for doing it.

Getting feedback after the action is accomplished is the best gift a coach or any person can receive! If this process of people reading can be done by an inexperienced learner with a total stranger, think what you can do to reach your team member at a whole new level. Be gentle, be careful not to interrogate the person, and do practice silence at the right times. Then watch a breakthrough happen!

YOUR JOURNEY: A Call to Action

Choose someone you don't know and practice people reading. Use the process above to guide you as you create a safe conversation through asking questions, listening in, feeding back what you heard the person say, and moving the person to a new level of awareness and problem-solving.

Great coaching comes from the heart, not the head.

– HERB KELLEHER, FORMER CEO, SOUTHWEST AIRLINES

Convey Support: The Coach's Role as Encourager

We all need someone who believes in us, inspires us, and helps us believe "yes, I can!" This is an important role of a coach. It's one of the reasons athletes and others work with a coach or like to play on a team with a coach who teaches and pushes, yet encourages too. It's a human need to know we are on the right path, doing "it" correctly or learning the right way to do something. Even if you've not completely mastered the skill, it's encouraging to know you have part of it right so far.

The word "courage" comes from the Latin word "curo," meaning "heart," and it's a word people use in so many ways. For instance, there are literally hundreds of songs with the word "heart" in the title. Consider these:

- "Shape of My Heart" by the Backstreet Boys.
- "Total Eclipse of the Heart" by Bonnie Tyler.
- "Heartbreak Hotel" by Elvis Presley.
- "My Heart Will Go On" by Celine Dion (the theme from the movie "Titanic")

We also refer to heart in various words and sayings: the heart of the matter, kind hearted, with all my heart, search your heart, learn it by heart, fainthearted, heartbroken, foolish heart, and heartburn. God used this powerful word when calling King David "a man after my own heart."

Heart means the vital center of one's being and emotions, the innermost part of self. Heart refers to love and affection for someone. Any way you view it, the heart is the essence, the center, the innermost part of a person. To be an encourager as a coach, then, is to have heart, to give heart, to speak with heart, and to listen with heart.

CASE IN POINT

I live in Louisville, Kentucky, home of the Kentucky Derby. It's the largest civic festival in the country, hosting multiple events over two weeks, ending with the famed Kentucky Derby horse race on the first Saturday in May.

One of the largest events is the Marathon and miniMarathon that takes place the Saturday before Derby. People come from around the world to experience this event and to run either the 26.2- or 13.1-mile historic race.

Not being a runner, but not wanting to miss the excitement, I've periodically gone to the race and placed myself somewhere along the route or even at the finish line, handing out cups of water and cheering on the runners.

It's amazing to watch the change in energy of the runners when they hear the shouts and cheers: "Come on, you can do it!" "Just one more mile; you've almost there." "We're praying for strength for you!" "You are strong and brave."

And when I know the person, and shout their name, it's even more meaningful for the runner: "Come on, Ted, you've done it before. Do it again!" "Way to go Chuck!" "Go, April, we're here for you!"

Even more powerful is the sweet voice of a child shouting and waving a banner that says, "Hi, Mommy. I love you!" Mommy's steps always become just a bit higher and stronger at that moment.

People can fear change, new ideas, and even their own growth. Stepping out into new territory can mentally bring a person back to the insecurity of first grade. Be an encourager. Let your team member know specifically what you believe about him. Affirm her specifically, rather than with a general comment. Let him know you appreciate his full engagement in the process. Tell her she's a joy to work with because she always greets you with a "good morning" in a cheerful tone of voice. And do say it with all your heart!

Leave every coaching encounter on a positive note. Make sure the person is affirmed and inspired to take action, believing that indeed they can. In his book *Masterful Coaching*, Robert Hargrove says he wants his clients to always leave him believing: "Anything is possible. Every situation is transformable. There is always a path forward, and the actions are up to you."

YOUR JOURNEY: A Call to Action

Consider a team member you are currently coaching. What do you appreciate or respect about him? What can you say that will encourage him to keep going? How could you celebrate the progress of your team member who's all in and growing so well?

*Unless commitment
is made, there are
only promises
and hopes …
but no plans.*

**– PETER F. DRUCKER,
PIONEER OF MODERN MANAGEMENT THEORY**

14

Obtain Commitment

People mean well. We really intend to do what we say. In our humanness we just don't always do it. Even the apostle Paul when speaking to the Romans centuries ago said, "I know what to do, and I don't do it. I know what not to do, and I do it anyway."

Commitment is the "I will." It's not "I think I can" or "maybe I'll do it" or "I'll try to do it." It's the unwavering "I'm all in, and I will." I find I usually need to lead and coach people to that place of understanding, commitment, action, and accountability. It's not always a natural way of thinking. A coach needs to help people think and act on purpose.

Commitment in the coaching sense relates to you, the coach, and the team member you are coaching. Remember the process shared in the story above that took place with Matt in the restaurant? Let's use that same process in the work environment as you coach your team member to a place of commitment.

CASE IN POINT

Sophia is a bright, experienced executive in a complex health care organization. Recently another area of work was added to her current responsibilities. This has been stressful for Sophia as she now has to juggle even more activities. Getting a handle on all that needs to be managed and done has been a challenge.

Sophia tends to be a detailed person, so she mostly had an eye on all the tasks that needed to be done. She was getting stuck in the weeds and not seeing the bigger picture of these new responsibilities. The feedback from her 360 survey validated this and also indicated that she needed to think bigger and to see the issues from a higher level. This was not natural or comfortable for Sophia, so she had to begin to see her additional work through a new lens.

Sophia admitted that she tended to over-contemplate issues, which caused her most of her stress. She would ruminate on decisions and get stuck in what to do.

The goal in coaching Sophia, then, was to help her see the bigger impact she could make by thinking at a higher level and making thoughtful decisions quicker.

Here is how our conversation went.

"Sophia, I heard you say you recognized that you need to figure out how to make a bigger impact in your department, think at a higher level, and not be in so much detail," I said. "Is that correct?"

"Yes, I need to do that," she replied.

"You said you NEED to do that. Do you also WANT to do that, Sophia?"

"Definitely, I need and want to make a bigger impact and think at a higher level and get out of the weeds."

"Do you have some ideas as to what 'a bigger impact' would look like?"

"Not completely, but I can figure it out."

"When do you plan to figure that out?"

"I'm so covered up right now. I'll get to it in the next few weeks."

"What would it take for you to set a specific date to work on this idea and define what that 'bigger impact' looks like?"

"Well, OK," she said while taking out her calendar. "I guess I could use my reflection time next week to work on this. Then I could have this better defined by August 14."

"OK, so I'm hearing that August 14 is your deadline to have this concept of the 'bigger impact' defined. Is that correct? Is that a commitment?"

"Yes, that's a commitment. I will have clearly defined what the bigger picture looks like and how I can make a bigger impact in this area. I'm putting it in my calendar right now!"

This is an easy process to help your team member be specific and work with dates to assure projects are started and completed. In Chapter 18, I'll discuss how you can take your team member to the next level of accountability for the commitment.

YOUR JOURNEY: A Call to Action

Over the past few chapters, you've learned about the Coach's Crown and the five C's of communication in the coaching process. Review the comments below on each of the C's and rate yourself on a scale of 1 to 10 on the comments.

Demonstrate Care: Score _____

"You Gotta Wanna." Are you genuinely interested in others' growth and building leaders? Do you have self-confidence enough to allow someone to grow beyond you? How well can you step back and allow the person to shine? Can you move your ego out of the way? Do you come from love, compassion, and reverence for people?

If you are not a 10 now, what would it take to become a 10?

_____

_____

_____

_____

_____

Have Clarity of Purpose: Score _____
Considering the person you are currently coaching, do you know the outcomes she wants and expects? Are your own intentions for this communication process clear? Are you there to help, guide, mentor, or teach? What's the purpose of the coaching? Is it to prepare the person for a new role? Build visibility in the organization? Help them see a blind spot? Prevent mistakes you made? Correct a performance issue?

If you are not a 10 now, what would it take to become a 10?

_____

_____

_____

_____

_____

Make a Connection: Score _____

How are you at building a relationship with the person? Are you aware of how to approach the person about the issue/process or have they approached you? How deep is your knowledge of the art, science, and complexity of communication? How well do you use the art of processing a person to get to their core criteria: asking power questions, using focused listening to build trust, giving feedback that can be heard, reading subtle signals and natural styles of people? Managing silence? Curiosity?

Do you project a positive presence when coaching?

Visual: Are you tuned into facial expressions, such as the power of a smile and soft expressions? Is your posture one of attention? Are your body movements and gestures welcoming? Are you aware of distractions and how they kill connection?

Vocal: Is your tone of voice, pitch, speed, and volume welcoming?

Verbal: Do you notice and listen for choice of words, remembering that language creates feelings and that feelings spark behavior. Are you learning to be comfortable managing silence? Are you speaking less and listening more?

If you are not a 10 now, what would it take to become a 10?

_____

_____

_____

_____

_____

Convey support: Score _____

Are you an encourager? How well can you work from your team member's goals, not yours? People can fear change, new ideas, and even growth. Stepping out to new territory can bring a person back to feeling like it's first grade; they can feel insecure. Are you nonjudgmental of their choices? Do you affirm him and celebrate his progress?

If you are not a 10 now, what would it take to become a 10?

_____

_____

_____

_____

_____

Obtain Commitment: Score _____

How well can you lead a person to a place of commitment and action? Are you able to move a person from "I want to" to "I will?"

If you are not a 10 now, what would it take to become a 10?

_____

_____

_____

_____

_____

_____

PART IV

Five Core Skills for Producing Extraordinary Results

No matter how great your attitude and how knowledgeable you are, you still need the skills, the "how to," when coaching a team member. In this last part of the coaching process, we'll take a look at the five core skills you need to master to lead your team member into their success zone. Each skill builds on the one before, yet all five skills are intertwined to create masterful thinking and action.

1. Asking questions.
2. Listening in.
3. Giving feedback.
4. Asking for new outcomes.
5. Holding people accountable.

*Answers put an end
to conversations;
questions ignite them.*

– RON SHAICH, FOUNDER, CEO PANERA BREAD

Questions: The Jewel in the Coach's Crown!

**REASONS WHY PEOPLE
HAVE TROUBLE ASKING QUESTIONS**

Have you noticed that most of us seem to believe the most important person in our life is ourselves? Many of us love to talk about ourselves, don't we? Let someone ask you one question, and generally you are off and running.

On the flip side of the coin, however, is our challenge with asking questions of other people. Are we so focused on ourselves that we don't think of others? Are we curious enough to explore what someone else thinks, feels, has done, or wants to do?

Those may be some of the reasons, but there are definite barriers that also keep you from asking questions of others and may include:

- **Asking questions can be risky.** "I don't know what the answer will be. I don't know how a question will be received."
- **You are in a hurry.** "Is my question going to open up a long conversation? I don't have time for that."
- **You lack the skills.** "I don't want to seem like I'm

interrogating a person. What happens after I ask a question and get a one-word answer? Now I have to ask another, and I'm not sure what to say. I'm not clear HOW to ask the question."

- **You lack curiosity.** "I'm too busy getting things done and focusing on my to-do list. Curiosity is not on my agenda."
- **You work in a culture that doesn't foster growth and curiosity.** "My organization runs a tight ship. We all multitask and have dual roles and responsibilities. Making time to explore another person or their reasons for doing something just doesn't fit with us."

Another thought here: Just because a person is more verbal and outgoing doesn't mean they are skilled in asking questions and building relationships. The quietest introvert can be excellent at asking questions, listening, and making connections with others.

Sometimes you put walls up not to keep people out, but to see who cares enough to break them down.

– Socrates

CASE IN POINT

Many years ago my pastor, Bob Russell, shared important points in a sermon about how we rush in and judge people without really knowing what's behind their decisions or behaviors. We not only judge in our heads but also often complain to someone else. He made a profound statement that has stayed with me over 20 years and that I've shared in many speeches and seminars since then: "Assume positive intentions while checking out the facts."

We do rush to judgement sometimes, don't we? We assume we know why a person does something. For example, a client shared this story.

Linda was a department head in radiology in a large hospital. She had a key staff person, Lucy, who was responsible for transporting patients to radiology for testing. She was kind and compassionate with patients, and everyone spoke kindly of Lucy. However, Lucy was regularly five to 10 minutes late to work and always left exactly at 3 p.m. when her shift ended. She always apologized when late but never gave a reason for her tardiness. Everyone was so busy that no one asked her.

Linda found herself complaining about this in her head and was quite judgmental about Lucy. She fussed about her to other department heads and was about to write her up for this offense. One time when Linda was complaining about Lucy, a colleague asked her why Lucy was late so often. Then Linda realized she'd never asked Lucy. She was very busy, with barely a minute to spare in her day, and was never curious enough to ask.

When Linda finally discussed this situation with Lucy, Lucy explained she was a single mother with a special-needs child whom she took to a small group home each morning. Generally, the home was open at 6:30 a.m., and she could drop off her son and get to work on time. But sometimes there was a delay because of weather or because the people caring for her son were late. That, then, made her a bit late to work.

Linda told me how embarrassed she was when she heard

this story. She was full of remorse that she didn't take the time and wasn't curious enough to ask Lucy why she was periodically late. She just assumed, erroneously, that Lucy was not a good time manager.

Linda has since upped her curiosity and continuously works on "assuming positive intentions while she checks out the facts" before judging someone's attitude or behavior.

FIVE LEVELS OF QUESTIONS

Leadership is not as much about knowing the right answers as it is about knowing the right questions.
– Bob Tiede, author of *Great Leaders Ask Questions*

Every question doesn't work or isn't appropriate in every situation. Sometimes you need a simple yes or no response. Sometimes you need explanation. Sometimes you need to go deeper and find out the real issue. As a coach to your team, it's helpful if you know and understand all five levels of questions and when to use them. They move from simple, safe questions to deeper, more sensitive questions.

Safe Questions draw out information and relax the other person. Generally, they are easy and effortless to answer. Safe questions make the person feel comfortable with you. Their responses don't require deep thought or analysis. Example: "How was your weekend, Joe?"

Closed questions are true/false, yes/no, or multiple-choice questions. They request a one- or two-word response. They are valuable for obtaining specific facts and enable you to control the conversation. However, used exclusively, they can make people feel interrogated. Example: "Did you finish the report?" Suggested beginnings for closed questions include "are," "do," "who," "where," and "which."

Open questions are like essay questions, allowing the individual to elaborate. They cause the person to continue to share. They increase a person's energy and often uncover a person's hot button. Example: "What results did you get from that research?" Suggested beginnings for open questions include "what," "how," and "in what way."

Interview questions zero in on a particular area or topic. They are more in depth and allow you to get closer to the person. They cause values to emerge, and you learn more about what a person believes. They are more intellectual than feeling. Example: "Where did you grow up, Steve?"

Congruent questions are sensitive, on target, and often cause great self-disclosure and breakthrough. They involve the feelings and emotions and bring about connection and relationships. Example: "What thoughts and feelings did that conversation spark in you, John?" Congruent questions are not always comfortable. However, with trust, patience, managing silence, and a high level of skill, the person will continue to respond. It's best to ask this type of questions after rapport is built.

POWER COACHING QUESTIONS

Telling creates resistance. Asking creates relationships.

— Andrew Sobel, coauthor of *Power Questions*

When coaching a team member, consider congruent questions when you want to:

- Build awareness and help your team member see an issue through a new lens.
  "Are you open to a suggestion to see this differently?"
- Create new ideas.
  "What would it look like if …?"
- Shift the conversation to the other person.
  "Thanks for asking. How do you see the situation?"
- Focus the conversation on the right issues.
  "Let's get back to the budget. What else do you need from me to get the information to the CFO by Monday?"
- Create deep, personal knowledge.
  "When did you first become aware of this fear?"
- Bring out feelings and emotions, not just ideas.
  "What part of that conversation causes you to feel angry?"
- Change behavior.
  "What would it take for you to …?"
- Touch on core values of the person.
  "How did you come to believe that?"

Note: If you already know the answer, it's not a power question; it's a leading question.

FAVORITE QUESTIONS TO UNDERSTAND OTHERS' GOALS

Here are a few of my favorite questions to help better understand what your team member is interested in, what she wants to work toward, and how serious she is to work the coaching process with you:

- Would you please tell me your story?
- What would you like to focus on?

- What's going on that makes you want to focus on that?
- What new skill would you like to learn or develop?
- What specific goal would you like to accomplish in the next six months?
- On a scale of 1 to 10, with 1 being "not at all" and 10 being "I'm all in," how motivated are you to achieving this goal?
- What would it take to turn that 6 (or whatever score she gives) into a 10?
- What would a celebration look like when you achieve this goal?
- What obstacles would keep you from accomplishing that?
- What would it take to …?

QUESTIONS TO STIMULATE THOUGHT

The greatest compliment that was ever paid me was when one asked me what I thought, and attended to my answer.
– Henry David Thoreau in his essay "Life Without Principle"

- What's working for you right now?
- What's not working?
- Tell me more.
- How would that work?
- What are your alternate choices?
- What are you afraid of?
- What are you passionate about?
- What are you really good at and still want to get better at?
- What area might you be stuck in and need new eyes to help you get unstuck?

The important thing is not to stop questioning.
Curiosity has its own reason for existing.
– Albert Einstein

THE POWER OF ASKING QUESTIONS OF YOURSELF

To continue to increase self-awareness, it's important to regularly ask yourself questions. My favorite questions at the end of the day are:

- What went well today?
- What could I have done differently today?
- Who did I serve today?

Journaling both the questions and the answers leads to new opening and learning. For instance, asking yourself what went well today gives you the opportunity to affirm yourself. Consequently, your confidence increases, and you are more likely to do this again. It's anchored in your mind.

When asking yourself what you could have done differently today, you'll pick up on small or big things that didn't quite go as you would have liked. Recognizing these situations gives you the opportunity to do it differently next time, or to go back and make amends when appropriate. It's best not to ask yourself what went wrong, as that creates a mindset of judging yourself. These questions are not about judging yourself. They are for reflection and learning.

As a growing servant leader, how about asking yourself who you served this day? Your response to yourself will keep you on the path of thinking about and living the life of a servant leader.

Other examples of self-questions that are good for awareness and growth are:

- What brought me joy today?
- What was going on that caused me to respond critically to John in the meeting today?
- How well did I manage my time today?
- How well did I honor my boundaries today, saying "yes" and "no" appropriately?
- How was my language today? Was I specific in my conversations? Did any of my words come across as judgmental?
- Did I eat mindfully today? When?

Your Journey: A Call to Action

What, specifically, was a key point of learning for you in the questions section?

_____

_____

_____

_____

On a scale of 1 to 10, rate yourself on the following.
Your comfort level of asking different kinds of questions:
Score _____

Your skill level of knowing what questions to ask and when:
Score _____

If you are not a 10 now, what would it take to become a 10?

_____

_____

*Coaching happens
not in your speaking,
but in your listening.*

– ELIZABETH JEFFRIES

Listening In:
Being Present to Serve

My wonderful mother, Catherine Nardi, always taught me the importance of listening well. She was famous for saying, "God gave you two ears and one mouth. That was His clue to listen twice as much as you talk."

THREE LEVELS OF LISTENING

You may not have thought that listening has three levels. You may think listening is simply focusing on the other person and, well, just listening to what they are saying! However, look at it this way. Listening is complex. Much is going on in a conversation. Our minds wander. We get easily distracted by something else that needs to be done. Or something in the room draws our attention. Or we're even distracted by something the person is wearing. Here are the three levels of listening that are going on simultaneously.

Level 1: Self-Talk. There are two people in your head: One is listening and talking with a real person, and one is talking with yourself. While you are listening, you may be saying to yourself, "That's a good thought" or "I totally disagree," or perhaps you go on a mental vacation and the person in your head is saying, "I'd like to go out to dinner tonight." It could be almost anything, but rest assured, there is a conversation going on inside as well as outside.

Level 2: The Content. You are in conversation with a person, and they have something they want to share with you, such as a message or a subject of some sort. The team member you are coaching may be telling you a story about what went well yesterday or what they learned. What the person is sharing with you is content.

Level 3: Listening Between the Lines. While the person is talking, you are consciously or unconsciously picking up on their energy, mood, tone of voice, fears, hopes, and enthusiasm. Perhaps the person starts to say something and stops. This is called self-filtering, and you wonder what they were about to say. You also may detect the language they are using. Are they all tied up, struggling, trying? In Level 3 you are evaluating the person and the message. Meaning is often made in the space between words.

> *The most important thing in communication*
> *is hearing what isn't said.*
> – Peter F. Drucker

POWER POINTS OF LISTENING

My friend, one of the pioneers in communication and listening skills, Robert Conklin, gave me permission many years ago to adapt, update, and share the following ideas from his book *How to Get People to Do Things*. These ideas are so helpful when coaching your team members or when engaged in any conversation.

Listening is a skill that can be learned. It takes practice and patience and focus. As with any skill, you need to care enough to work on it, which is why "want to listen" is the first power point. Here's the complete list:

- **Want to listen.** Almost all problems in listening can be overcome by having the right attitudes. Remember that there is no such thing as uninteresting people, just uninterested listeners.

- **Act like a good listener.** Be alert, sit straight, lean forward if appropriate, and let your face radiate interest.

- **Listen to understand.** Don't just listen for the sake of listening; listen to gain a real understanding of what is being said.

- **React.** The only time a person likes to be interrupted is when she is being applauded. Be generous with your applause. Make the other person feel important. Applaud with nods, smiles, comments, or encouragement.

- **Stop talking.** You can't listen while you are talking. Communicate; don't take turns talking. Don't interrupt. Allow the person to finish their thought.

- **Ask questions.** When you don't understand, when you need further clarification, when you want to show you are listening, ask questions.

- **Concentrate on what the other person is saying.** Actively focus your attention on the words, the ideas, and the feelings related to the subject.

- **Look at the other person.** Pay attention to his face, mouth, eyes, hands, body language. That will all help the other person communicate with you and will help you read what they might not be saying.

- Get rid of distractions. Put down any papers, pencils, phone, etc. Turn away from your computer if you are in your office.
- Share responsibility for communication. Only part of the responsibility rests with the speaker; you as the listener have an important part. Seek to understand, and if you don't, ask for clarification.

YOUR JOURNEY: A Call to Action

On a scale of 1 to 10, rate yourself on the following.

Active Listening: **Score** _____

How well can you focus on the person without your mind wandering? Can you avoid constant interruptions to make your own point? How well can you read the subtle signals that let you know what the person may be thinking? Can you listen between the lines to detect hopes, fears, enthusiasm?

If you are not a 10 now, what would it take to become a 10?

_____

_____

_____

_____

_____

_____

Feedback:
The Gift of Growth

*Leaders cannot work in a vacuum. They may take on larger,
seemingly more important, roles in an organization, but this
does not exclude them from asking for and using feedback.*
– Jack Canfield, Coauthor, *Chicken Soup for the Soul* Series

G iving and getting feedback is critical to the coaching
process! Your team member can't grow without
feedback from you and others. This is where the
mirror is held up, and he sees himself through the lens of
others. Hopefully, he's experienced the 360-degree survey I
discussed in Chapter 3 and has been debriefed on the results.
Most likely those were also used to help in setting goals for
the coaching process.

It's often difficult to give feedback to others, including a
person you are coaching. That's why I always ask the same
question before I offer feedback. I need to know if they want
feedback, if they are just venting or talking to hear themselves,
or if they want possible solutions.

Everyone isn't open to feedback, and you need to know
clearly what their expectations are. For instance, you can ask,

"Are you open to feedback on this situation?" or "Would you like feedback on this issue, or do you want me to listen?" or possibly "Are you open to my thoughts and insights?"

REASONS WHY PEOPLE AVOID GIVING FEEDBACK TO OTHERS

- **Lack of skills:** You haven't fully developed the skills of asking questions, listening, sharing expectations, asking for what you want, staying the course, setting boundaries, or holding people accountable with consequences.
- **Fear:** You fear rejection because you want people's approval. You think, "What if he doesn't like what I have to say?" or "What if she says negative things to other people about my feedback?"
- **Lack of language:** You lack the language to express yourself, so you don't attempt feedback. You are concerned you'll sound judgmental and righteous.
- **You're a mind reader:** You think people can read your mind and know what you want! You think, "Why do I have to give feedback? She should know what I want."
- **Lack of confidence:** You lack confidence in yourself to give feedback, and you don't completely trust the process. You think, "What if I stick my neck out to say something, and it's not received well?"

What you permit, you promote!
– Elizabeth Jeffries

You've seen me mention the words above previously in this book: "What you permit, you promote." I've used that saying for years, thanks to a participant in a teaming session I facilitated at a hospital in Alabama.

I was working with a leadership team of a hospital, and we were discussing how to get people to follow up on what they said they'd do and what to do about people who don't. In discussing consequences, the team agreed how difficult it was to decide on consequences and hold people to them.

Just then a brilliant team member said, "If a person is not performing the way you need them to perform and you let them continue to do what they've been doing, you are really saying it's OK. What you permit, you promote!"

So there it is – the truth, the powerful statement that gets you in trouble every time! You lose the right to fuss about something or someone if you don't address it. For sure, what you permit, you promote!

YOUR JOURNEY: A Call to Action

On a scale of 1 to 10, rate yourself on the following.

Giving Feedback: The gift of growth: **Score** _____

Can you speak the truth in love to someone and give honest feedback? Do you have the confidence to give honest feedback? Do you have the skills and language to express yourself so that the person hears you? Are you fussing about a behavior or attitude of a team member but not addressing it with them?

_____

_____

If you are not a 10 now, what would it take to become a 10?

_____

_____

*When we fail
to set boundaries
and hold people accountable,
we feel used and mistreated.
This is why we sometimes
attack who they are,
which is far more hurtful
than addressing a
behavior or a choice.*

**– BRENE BROWN, AUTHOR AND RESEARCHER
ON VULNERABILITY AND SHAME**

Asking for New Outcomes and Holding People Accountable: The Final Steps on the Road to Results

THE SEVEN-STEP ACCOUNTABILITY SCRIPT

Throughout this book, I've shared ideas, insights, and techniques on how to connect with the person you are coaching. I'm certain by now you can see the importance of questions and why they are the jewel in the Coach's Crown. Combining great questions with active listening skills and feedback, you'll accomplish amazing success as a coach, and your team member will grow further into their success zone.

However, the real key to helping your team member to excel is to lead her, through questions and listening in, to reach clear commitments and then help her be accountable for specific results. Did you notice that many of the Case in Point stories included accountability?

To give you a clear picture of this full process, I've created a simple script to guide you. The Seven-Step Accountability Script will guide you through the process from Step 1, describing the situation you observe, all the way to Step 7, getting agreement to take action with accountability for results.

EXAMPLE SCRIPT

Preparation: Consider a situation with a team member that you would like to address. It's important to be clear in your own mind what it is and what you are willing to commit to in time, knowledge, and energy to develop this person. Prepare yourself mentally and approach the person with an attitude of serving and helping to develop them to their next level of growth.

Team member: Kevin Johnson

Coaching Situation: Kevin has been with the organization for four years. His team says he's been easy to work with, a really nice guy who gets his work done on time. Other feedback indicated Kevin is vague in his communication and sometimes it isn't clear exactly what he expects. His team would like him to be more clear and specific in his communication.

1. **Describe** the person's specific behavior/attitude/ skill objectively.
   "I've noticed, Kevin, that you are a good thinker and full of optimism about what we can accomplish in our department. You've taken on projects, moved issues through on time, and had good results. I think you have potential to grow further as a leader here.

2. **Express** your feelings and thoughts about his behavior.
   "I have noticed some hesitation in your dealings with people and asking for what you need in a way that the

team will follow you. You seem to have less confidence in that area." (Include your feelings of mad, sad, glad, or scared when appropriate.)

3. **Question** what may be going on with the person, what are they thinking, what would they like to do about this, etc. "Does any of this ring true to you, Kevin? Do you see what your team means?" (Kevin responds that, yes, he sees this and realizes this is a gap.) "Would you like to have some help to develop yourself in this area and learn specific skills that will help you communicate and lead more effectively?" (Kevin says that, yes, he'd appreciate help.)

4. **Suggest** new possibilities, a different approach. "I'd be thrilled to coach you in that area if it's of interest to you, Kevin. I'm willing to set up a way to do this over the next few months. I can offer insights and suggestions to help you grow."

5. **Explain** the benefits to Kevin that will result from the new behavior, attitude, or skills. Appeal to his needs/wants. "Developing communication skills will accelerate your career path, Kevin. We are doing succession planning in the company, and there could be some good opportunities for you in the future."

6. **Ask** for a commitment to the offer. "Kevin, in agreeing to coaching, I'd like you to experience a few leadership/communication assessments, so you will know more about yourself, and I can know more about you. Also, please identify up to three goals you'd like to accomplish or three areas you'd like to grow in over the next three months. Will this work for you?" (Kevin is excited and says yes.)

The next part of the process is the key to ensuring there is action with results. This is where you will need to ask several questions to lead Kevin to specific commitments with a time factor. Most people aren't used to this, so keep gently asking questions until you get specific closure.

7. **Account** for their commitment through a specific date/deadline.

   "OK, Kevin, please contact Mary in HR to send you a link to take the assessments. Then will you please send me the three goals or issues you'd like to work on over the next three months?" (Kevin says, "Yes, I will do this.") "How will I know you've completed this, Kevin?" (Kevin says, "I'll let you know.") "Specifically, Kevin, when will you let me know?" (Kevin says he'll have the goals to you by the end of the day Friday. He agrees to contact Mary this afternoon for the assessment link and complete the assessment first thing tomorrow morning.)

PRACTICE THE SEVEN-STEP ACCOUNTABILITY SCRIPT

Preparation: Decide on a person who could benefit from short-term coaching with you. It's important to be clear in your own mind what it is and what you are willing to commit to in time, knowledge, and energy to develop this person.

Prepare yourself mentally and approach the person with an attitude of serving and helping to develop them to their next level of growth. Play with the script below until you are comfortable with the process and questions. Then approach the person and, assuming they will give a strong yes, go on with coaching your team member to new success!

Team member:

Coaching Situation:

1. **Describe:** What is the opportunity for developmental coaching you've observed, or what are the issues or goals you've been asked to address to help a team member?
2. **Express:** What are your feelings and thoughts about it? Mad? Sad? Glad? Scared?
3. **Question:** What questions do you want to ask or issues to explore?
4. **Suggest:** What new outcomes do you want or would like to explore as a coach?
5. **Explain:** What are the benefits to the person?
6. **Ask:** What will you say to ask for a commitment?
7. **Account for:** What will you say to hold the person accountable?

DEVELOPING PEER-TO-PEER ACCOUNTABILITY PARTNERSHIPS

When you're coaching a team member, it's also very helpful for the team member to choose a person in your organization as an accountability partner. This could be a colleague, a peer, or just a good friend in the organization whom they trust. While they are certainly accountable to you for the commitments they've made in the coaching process, this one is a different type of relationship. It's also one with a different timetable.

For instance, suppose you meet with your team member every few weeks for six months or so, focusing on up to three issues/situations they want to work through. Ideally, in an accountability partnership, the timeframe is 60 or 90 days, and the goals/issues worked through are more specific and focused. It may be just one goal, but it is connected to the overall goals in the coaching process. Also, both partners participate and share specific goals.

There's a huge benefit to the second partner, especially if they are not in a coaching relationship. They become more aware of goals, the need for goals, and the need for celebration of accomplishments. This type of partnership is more collegial and informal, but the purpose is still to help each partner accomplish something specific.

In the three-month summary of my coaching client, Jason, he said the following about his accountability partnership with Cindy: "As part of the coaching experience, we were asked to have an accountability partner in house. Cindy and I paired up for this, and it has been a great experience. Knowing each other and having worked with each other in the past allowed us to make this very effective immediately. We are very open with one another, and we are both willing to tell the other what we need to hear, but might not want to hear. She has certainly helped hold me accountable for what I said I'd do."

SUGGESTED PEER-TO-PEER ACCOUNTABILITY PARTNERSHIP PROCESS

To make accountability partnerships work to the maximum, there are several points to consider. It will work beautifully if both partners are fully invested, have SMART goals, and keep the communication going for the specified length of time. If the criteria below are met, great goals can be accomplished!

1. "Ya gotta wanna." Make a personal commitment to one or two goals that entail change or growth. Focus on areas of

importance to you that you can get excited about and are linked to your coaching process.

2. Choose a partner in your organization whom you know and trust who is also committed and has an interest in growing or changing something in their lives or work.

3. Share your goals with each other.

4. Decide on a length of time for the partnership: 30 days, 60 days, 90 days.

5. Agree on the type of communication.
   - How: In person, by phone, by email, by text. It's best to meet in person sometimes if at all possible.
   - How often: Once a week, perhaps at a specific day and time. (Or decide on the next meeting at the end of the current one.)
   - Where: A conference room, one of your offices, at lunch or coffee, etc.

6. The connection and how it works at each meeting
   - Partner #1: Restate your goal, the actions accomplished, the actions not accomplished, and why not.
   - Partner #2: Restate your goal, the actions accomplished, the actions not accomplished, and why not.
   - Affirm each other with specific statements such as, "That was really tough, and you plowed right through it. That took courage, and I'm thrilled you got the outcomes you wanted."
   - Commit to the goal(s) you will work toward for your next meeting.
   - Confirm your next communication/time of meeting and where.
   - Option: Email goals and accomplishments to each other before you meet.

6. Tell your family what you are doing and share what you are accomplishing to let them be cheerleaders for you.

THE BENEFIT OF SHORT-TERM PEER-TO-PEER ACCOUNTABILITY PARTNERSHIPS

Short-term accountability partnerships are energizing and can produce great personal and professional growth, as well as a positive impact on the organization. Here's what your team members will experience:

1. You will accomplish more because writing down goals crystallizes thought and leads to action.
2. Discussion and exchange of ideas will spark new ideas.
3. Short-term accountability partnerships are critical for helping chart progress. Writing down goals and checking off items on your list gives you a sense of accomplishment and satisfaction.

MANAGING YOURSELF IN THE ACCOUNTABILITY PROCESS

To assure the peer-to-peer accountability process is working, share these ideas with your team members. These small steps will bring great results.

- **Journal!** Ask yourself questions regularly throughout the day. It will increase your level of self-awareness and create the environment to think about what went well today and what you could have done differently.
- **Manage your self-talk.** Your brain doesn't know fact from fiction. You will tend to behave based on the messages you tell yourself. Be careful of the words you speak to yourself. Remember that language creates feelings, and feelings spark behavior.

- **Watch who you are spending time with!** Make sure they are positive uplifting people who encourage you and not drag you down. Stay away from negative, complaining people who want you to fail.

PEER-TO-PEER ACCOUNTABILITY PARTNERSHIP TEMPLATE

To help you be accountable for new outcomes, arrange follow-up with an accountability partner:

My accountability partner is _____ (name).

I will speak with him/her on _____ (date) at _____ (time).

His/her phone number/email is _____ .

You must do the thing you think you cannot do.
– Eleanor Roosevelt

MAKE LEARNING STICK

Bob Pike, master trainer of trainers, says, "Learning doesn't take place until behavior changes." To facilitate learning, then, and to make it stick, here are five steps to guide you.

Discovery. This is the "aha" phase where a person discovers or learns for the first time there are gaps or areas in their behavior or skills that need attention. The discovery phase is about awareness, and it's essential and foundational. Awareness precedes change. Nothing happens until you know something is awry. This may happen through the assessments or through questions from a coach.

Mary Ann was an experienced, capable leader, but she slid into a situation and habits that reduced her effectiveness. She didn't realize she had such a challenge with time management. She just assumed everyone was busy and overworked. She worked long hours, came in early, left late, and was more irritable lately. She lost her joy for work and didn't even realize it.

When her 360 survey pointed out that her team was concerned about her disorganization and late projects, Mary Ann became aware of the seriousness of this issue and saw how it was affecting her leadership and the productivity of the department.

Motivation. The word "motivation" means "to move to action." You'll never get action without desire. Remember that statement "you gotta wanna?" Nothing happens without motivation.

Mary Ann definitely wanted to be and be seen as a good leader. She was very concerned that her team had this view of her, and so she was motivated to do something about it.

Processing. This is the time for thinking it through, sorting it out, and figuring out the goal and the steps to achieve it.

A suggestion to Mary Ann was that she set aside some reflecting time and look at how she was scheduling her calendar and her to-do list. I also suggested she create a time log over a two-week period to see more clearly where she actually spent her time. Another idea was to ask her key staff to share insights into her time-mastery issues, so she would know more specifically what they saw needed attention.

Practice. Here's where you actually apply the ideas, methods, and beliefs regularly, over and over again. You repeatedly perform the skill to proficiency.

Mary Ann took this goal seriously. She clarified and renewed her vision for her department, so she had a target to shoot for. She shared it with her team and helped them revitalize too. Mary Ann wrote out a project to-do list for the week, and each day she planned which part of the work she would tackle. She used a tickler system for remembering when something was due or when she needed to help a team member be accountable for their work.

Mary Ann reviewed the competencies of her team members and reached out to them with projects to help them develop and grow. This way, she was coaching them in new skills and supporting their learning, rather than getting caught in the weeds of trying to do everything herself.

Feedback. Now it's time to check in with a few people to learn what they see and hear as a result of these steps. Do they experience you differently? If so, how?

This was the most exciting time for Mary Ann! Her focus and hard work were paying off. In just a few months, she was much more organized, relaxed, and playful with her team, and her department overall was much more productive. She didn't even have to specifically ask her team for feedback. They offered it willingly. They knew Mary Ann was being coached and working on her time mastery, and when they saw positive outcomes, they couldn't help but affirm her regularly.

In a six-month process, your team member has time for action and feedback and can experience real progress. That in itself is motivating and helps the person to stay the course and continue to grow and build new habits.

YOUR JOURNEY: A Call to Action

On a scale of 1 to 10, rate yourself on the following.

Asking for new outcomes: **Score** _____

Do you know the outcomes you want/expect? Are you skilled in articulating the outcomes you expect? Are you willing to ask for what you want and have the language and confidence to ask?

_____

_____

If you are not a 10 now, what would it take to become a 10?

_____

_____

_____

_____

Holding people accountable for their commitments: **Score** _____

Can you hold people accountable for what they agreed to do? Are there consequences if they miss deadlines/dates? Do you know the questions to ask to help them be accountable?

_____

_____

_____

If you are not a 10 now, what would it take to become a 10?

_____

_____

_____

_____

Let him who would move the world, first move himself.

– GALILEO GALILEI

Developing Yourself as You Coach Others

My first coach, Bill McGrane, told me you can't give away what you don't have, so be a lifelong learner, stretch yourself, try new things, and allow yourself to be uncomfortable!

If you want to be a good coach, start with knowing and growing yourself. The ancient Greek aphorism "know thyself" is so very true. Be introspective, ask for feedback from others, be honest with yourself, and learn and practice new skills.

Before you take on a more intentional role of a coach to a team member, it's important that you have been coached yourself for at least several months and also that you've been part of an accountability partnership for several months. These experiences will be invaluable to you as you sit in a different chair and coach your team from another viewpoint. You'll know more fully what you liked and what sparked you to take action and stay motivated. You'll also know what not to do that may turn off a team member you are coaching. There's nothing like learning and applying that learning from our own experiences!

Since any team member you are coaching will have

experienced the battery of validated assessments, it's important for you, as coach, to at least experience the communication and leadership behavior part yourself. By knowing your own style and preferences in communication and leadership behavior, you will more easily learn to flex and adapt to others.

See Deep Dive into Validated Assessments in the appendix for details and help on knowing yourself more fully through validated assessments.

ABOUT "SPEAKING THE TRUTH IN LOVE"

I've used the phrase "speak the truth in love" regularly in this book. People talk about speaking the truth to others, and it's important for sure. However, the last two words in the phrase – "in love" – are perhaps even more important. They tell us how to speak the truth to others. It's about choosing language, tone, facial expressions, and body language that are more easily received, especially when there's something tough to share.

Speaking the truth means having the courage to speak up about things that matter, even if they are little things that have big consequences.

CASE IN POINT

I have a friend who's been married a long time. Like most marriages, there are ups and downs. We all love to hear a man or a woman say something sweet and complimentary about their spouse, but it's most uncomfortable to hear a person say something derogatory about their spouse or put their spouse down, especially in front of others.

My friend loves her husband. Yet when we were together

doing girl things, she would put him down, criticize him for various things, and make fun of him. After several occasions I became more and more uncomfortable. I was sure she didn't realize the extent of her comments, and one day I decided I needed to speak the truth in love.

It was hard. Following what I'd been taught years ago, I stayed away from the accusing "you" words and softened my first comment with a question.

"Joan, are you open to hearing something I've observed in your communication?"

"Of course," she said.

"Joan, I know you love Tim. Lately I've heard you criticize him a great deal. I don't think you are aware of it or how uncomfortable it makes others feel when you say negative things about him. Does this ring true at all?"

Long pause from Joan. Silence from me.

"Really?" she said. "Oh my gosh, I had no idea! Actually, I really hate those kind of comments. My mother used to do that all the time when she talked about my father. I wonder if I heard it so much, and it's so deep in my mind that I don't realize what I'm saying. I'm so sorry. I need to apologize to Tim and to my friends because I love my husband, and I never want to portray him like that. Thank you for telling me. Only a true friend would tell me this."

WHAT IF?

Let's assume that Joan had responded defensively, or when you asked a question to address your observations, she had said, "No, I'm not open to hearing your observation."

First of all, in a personal friendship as described above, it's doubtful Joan would say no. However, in this situation, if she said she didn't want my observation, I would drop the conversation. I'd also trust she wasn't ready to hear the truth, or she may have guessed what I was about to say and didn't want to deal with it now. Either way, I would go no further. I would do my best to love her where she is and minimize the friendship if it became more uncomfortable. Lastly, I would take a look at my own need to fix the situation and ask myself some questions about that.

Let's assume this is a work situation with a peer who's not holding up their part of the workload as expected. If it's noticed by and affects other team members, someone needs to address it. Remember the phrase "what you permit, you promote?" Hopefully, the manager of this person will address it, but maybe not. In that case, the circumstances and preparation of addressing the situation are key. Go back through the accountability script and work out a script to speak the truth in love to this person. It's more likely to succeed if you have a relationship with the person. Check to make sure you know his story and the possible reasons he's not doing his work as expected. Here again, assume positive intentions while checking out the facts.

Lastly, let's assume you are the boss or the coach to someone, and a situation is unacceptable, so you decide to address it. It's highly unlikely that the person will say they don't want to hear your observations. You have positional power. If they get defensive or shut down on you, slow down, lower your voice, and gently share your observations of their body language or voice, like this: "John, it seems I hit a nerve by bringing this up. I've noticed you've stopped talking, and your body language shifted."

Then wait for a response because you will get something from this person. And take it gently from there. Remember that everyone has a story, and behind much defensiveness is fear. Follow the path and find out what's really going on. Patience, patience, patience!

When coaching, it's inevitable that you will see and hear language, comments, and issues that may be small but have big consequences. Are you willing to address them, to speak the truth in a kind way where the person can hear and digest what needs to be said?

END NOTE: THE REST OF THE STORY OF NANCY

Remember Nancy? She's the leader I told you about in the beginning of the book who was the ideal developmental coaching candidate. I worked with her for several months to help onboard her to her new role as vice president and COO.

A few years after that promotion, I received a call from the human resources department of that same health system. They were in a succession-planning process and wanted to know if I was available to help prepare Nancy for a possible CEO role. "My total pleasure," I said, knowing that Nancy was well equipped to be considered for this next executive role.

I talked with Nancy and made arrangements to meet to begin this new adventure. A short time later, I walked into Nancy's office, ready to work with her on new goals to help her prepare for the next assignment.

This is the part I love about change happening so fast! In the short time since we had talked, things sped up in the health system, and Nancy was just appointed CEO the day I arrived. Because Nancy is a brilliant achiever with amazing relationship skills, we jumped right into strategy and an onboarding process.

Today, Nancy is still CEO of that hospital, and the health system has grown and added many more facilities. I won't be surprised if one day soon I get a call that Nancy is about to be promoted again and would I come join her for another adventure.

CLOSING WISHES FOR YOU

I trust there have been key points in this book that have sparked you to look at leadership and coaching with a new lens. To think that someone opens their mind and their heart and allows you into their life and their work is humbling indeed. As a coach, there's nothing more rewarding than to be a little part of the successes of the people you've had the privilege of knowing and working with. It's worthy work and a true blessing.

My wish for you is that you will put on your Coach's Crown, stretch yourself out of your comfort zone, make a commitment, and start coaching a team member into her success zone today. It will be the most important work you'll ever do because the highest work of a leader is to develop more leaders. Go on! She's waiting for you!

What we call the beginning is often the end, and to make an end is to make a beginning. The end is where we start from.
— **T.S. Eliot**

Deep Dive Into Validated Assessments

I've set this section apart to give you specific, deeper insights into the five validated assessments I discussed earlier. These instruments are a powerful way to help you and your team members break through old perceptions and see yourselves though a new lens. As you do that, you'll be better able to understand others and create much more compatible relationships. Ultimately, good relationships and communication equal great outcomes!

Following is a description of the five sciences I recommend you incorporate into your coaching process with your team members. Let's take a deep dive into:

- Discovering your behavior style.
- Awakening your driving forces, your passions.
- Defining your core skills or competencies.
- Understanding your acumen, your decision-making ability.
- Unleashing your emotional intelligence.

Appendix A

Discovering Your Behavior Style

HOW YOU TEND TO BEHAVE AND YOUR ABILITY TO INTERACT WITH AND RESPOND TO OTHERS

Behavior is the way we act or conduct ourselves. It's our way of doing things. Behavior is visible, and it's what I like to call an "open loop." In other words, it affects other people.

Think about this: You have a circulatory system, and right now blood is rushing through your arteries away from your heart, bringing oxygen to your body. At the same time, your veins are carrying oxygen-poor blood back from the body to your heart to be cleaned up. Your circulatory system is a closed loop; what happens inside your body stays in your body and doesn't affect anyone else.

Communication and behavior, however, are open loops and can affect relationships in multiple ways. For instance, remember the time you walked past a group of people deeply engaged in play and laughter? You didn't have a clue what they were laughing about, but you couldn't help laughing along with them or at least putting on a big smile. That's open loop. What you experienced from other people caused a reaction from you.

Remember that negative-attitude person down the hall from you? It seemed to drag down your spirits just being around him or hearing his voice. Then there's that child or grandchild; one smile from that baby, and you are hooked and oh so joyful! That's a miraculous open loop, isn't it?

All of us are wired a certain way. But that doesn't mean you can't control or flex your natural style. A mature, wise person will learn to flex their behavior to meet the circumstances of the environment.

The four-style behavior model has been around since Hippocrates' time, described at that time in terms related to the fluids of the body: bile, blood, urine, and saliva. Next came the terms choleric, sanguine, phlegmatic, and melancholy. Researched and validated, in today's terms, we use the words Dominance, Influence, Steadiness, and Compliance, or what is known as the DISC model.

The four dimensions of behavior measure:

- How you tend to solve problems and meet challenges.
- How you tend to influence others to your point of view.
- How you tend to respond to the pace of the environment you are in.
- How you tend to respond to rules and procedures set by other people.

Everyone behaves within these four dimensions. It's the combination of these four dimensions and how they come together to create a pattern of how you personally tend to behave and, of course, how your behavior is received by others.

It's more than knowing your own style; it's also knowing how to interact with people of different styles. It's not judging them because they are different than you or laughing at them because they need time to think or criticizing them because they move so fast. You may not like or connect to a person's behavior, but you are not called to like each other. As Mother Teresa said, "We are called to love each other, and in so doing we can learn to adjust to our differences."

YOUR JOURNEY: Call to Action

Below are statements about how each of the dimensions tends to communicate or coach. Compare these to your own style and check which statement most describes you in all four dimensions.

DOMINANCE: How a person tends to respond to problems and challenges

___ I tend to take an active, assertive, direct approach to getting results. I tend to make quick decisions and tend to be impatient with others who move slower.

___ I tend to obtain results in a more organized, deliberate, and calculated way. I need information and to think about it before I decide.

INFLUENCE: How a person tends to influence others to their point of view

___ I tend to approach new people in an outgoing gregarious manner. I'm pretty talkative and can be impulsive and emotional. I need relationships.

___ I tend to approach new people in a friendly but reserved and logical manner. I need procedures and to know how things are done.

STEADINESS: How a person responds to the pace of the environment

I tend to prefer a more controlled deliberate, predictable environment. I listen well, and need safety and security.

I tend to prefer a more flexible, dynamic, unstructured environment. I'm more the "don't fence me in" type and need freedom of expression.

COMPLIANCE: How a person responds to rules and procedures set by others

I tend to prefer that things are done the "right way," according to the book or the established standards. I need accuracy.

I tend to operate more independently, feeling the right way is my way. I tend to bend or break rules if they don't make sense. I need freedom and change.

ADAPTING AND FLEXING STYLES

In the end, it's all about relationships.
— Elizabeth Jeffries

Once you've discovered your own predominant style of communication and leadership and that of the team member you are coaching, use the following guide to create an environment to help you communicate in a way they will hear you. The language of the four-style model is DISC, which stands for and measures Dominance, Influence, Steadiness, and Compliance.

Dominance. When communicating with a person who comes across as ambitious, forceful, decisive, strong-willed, independent, and goal-oriented:

- Be clear, specific, brief, and to the point.
- Stick to business.
- Be prepared with support material in a well-organized package.

The following factors may create tension or dissatisfaction for a person with this tendency:

- Talking about things that are not relevant to the issue.
- Leaving loopholes or cloudy issues.
- Appearing disorganized.

Influence. When communicating with a person who comes across as magnetic, enthusiastic, friendly, and demonstrative:

- Provide a warm and friendly environment.
- Don't deal with a lot of details. If needed, put them in writing.
- Ask "feeling" questions to draw out their opinions or comments.

The following factors may create tension or dissatisfaction for a person with this tendency:

- Being cold, curt, or uncommunicative.
- Controlling the conversation so they can't talk.
- Dwelling on facts and figures or abstractions.

Steadiness. When communicating with a person who is patient, predictable, reliable, steady, relaxed, and modest:

- Break the ice with a personal comment.

- Present your case softly and non-threateningly.
- Ask "how" questions to draw out their opinions.

The following factors may create tension or dissatisfaction for a person with this tendency:

- Rushing headlong into business.
- Being domineering or demanding.
- Forcing them to respond quickly to your objectives; they need time to think.

Compliance. When communicating with a person who is neat, conservative, perfectionist, careful, and compliant:

- Prepare your case in advance.
- Be accurate and realistic.
- Stick to business.

The following factors may create tension or dissatisfaction for a person with this tendency:

- Being giddy, casual, informal, loud.
- Pushing too hard or being unrealistic with deadlines.
- Being disorganized or messy.

YOUR JOURNEY: A Call to Action

List the names and probable behavior style of two of your team members who may be good coaching candidates.

_____

_____

_____

_____

_____

Appendix B

Awakening Your Driving Forces

**THE WHY OR THE DRIVERS BEHIND
YOUR ACTIONS AND YOUR PASSIONS**

Everyone is motivated. We're just not all motivated by the same things. The research of Eduard Springer tells us that everyone is driven by some combination of the six primary types of human motivation:

- Knowledge.
- Utility.
- Surroundings.
- Others.
- Power.
- Methodologies.

Each motivator can be looked at on a continuum between two extremes so that a person can better understand what really drives them in work and life. We all fall somewhere on the continuum for each of the six motivators.

YOUR JOURNEY: Call to Action

Can you identify where on the continuum you fall? (Choose one of each from types below.)

Knowledge. You are more

Intellectual – driven to discover truth and knowledge for knowledge's sake.

Instinctive – driven by relevant knowledge; using intuition and/or experience.

Utility. You are more:

Resourceful – driven by practical results, efficiency, and return on investment; wealth interests.

Selfless – driven to generously assist others with minimal expectation of personal return.

Surroundings. You are more:

Harmonious – driven by harmony and balance in surroundings and relationships; subjective.

Objective – driven and have the ability to compartmentalize in chaotic situations and focus on outcomes and function.

Others. You are more:

Altruistic: driven to give generously, serving others, with no expectation of personal return.

Intentional – driven to assist others in areas of personal interest, not for the sake of just helping.

Power. You are more:

_____ Commanding – driven to assert control over their freedom and destiny.

_____ Collaborative – driven by comfort in a supporting role, without need for recognition.

Methodologies. You are more:

_____ Structured –driven by a traditional approach, proven methods, and defined system for living.

_____ Receptive – driven to be open to new ideas, methods, and opportunities that fall outside the defined system.

When people understand their top driver and are placed in roles or projects that match their passion, they will soar! They will have a strong pull toward action. On the other hand, if placed in a role or project where there is indifference or maybe even avoidance, there's no energy for action, and progress will languish.

When a leader knows and affirms their team members' top drivers, they can place people in a role or assign a project that matches their passion and then watch them succeed. Knowing and understanding your passion and drive helps you to minimize judging other people. This knowledge broadens your perspective of your differences and builds acceptance versus conflict.

CASE IN POINT

For the past 15 years I've served on the board of Maryhurst, a 175-year-old nonprofit organization that cares for the highest needs children and families in the state of Kentucky. As part of my contribution to Maryhurst, I'll periodically provide learning programs for the leadership team of approximately 12 people. In assessing their leadership styles and drivers, it is no surprise that each of the team members scores highest on the Altruistic end of Others. Each of the team members has a drive to generously give to others. Not a one of them is in this very difficult work for money or fame. For them, it's all about serving others. They care, they give, and everything they do and talk about is serving our children and families.

Please note that their styles are all different. That's a good thing! On a team, you want differences in styles and similarities in motivators. It's no wonder that the turnover on Maryhurst's leadership team is so very low; many of these leaders have been at Maryhurst for 10 or 20 years or more! They work in an organization where their personal values are in alignment with the organization, and they work in a career where their drives and passions are being met. It just doesn't get much better than that!

CASE IN POINT

Some years ago, I was helping an engineering firm select an additional engineer for their team. One of the final candidates, Ron, was asked to experience our battery of assessments, including Behavior and Motivators. When I was debriefing the report with the CEO and COO on the phone, I explained that Ron's style was primarily Compliance with a backup of Steadiness. This was not unusual for someone in the profession of engineering, and he would be a detailed introvert with a low need for lots of communication. When it came to discussing Ron's motivators, I explained that Ron most likely did not work primarily for money, but was primarily interested in quality and service.

At this point, there was silence on the other end of the line. Confused, I waited a moment and then asked if they wanted me to repeat this information. They both laughed and told me about Ron at the interview. Apparently, Ron asked many questions about resources, a few about people and the expectations of the job, but never once asked about salary or benefits. When the CEO and COO explained the financial package, Ron simply said OK and moved on to another question about resources.

Yes, Ron wanted to be paid fairly, but money was not his primary driving force. So if money was the focus of these two leaders, it was not going to be a deciding factor for Ron to join this team. Ron was more interested in creating materials for quality construction work. They hired Ron, and to the best of my knowledge, he's still focusing on quality and service at this large construction company.

Appendix C

Defining Your Core Skills or Competencies

THE LEVEL OF DEVELOPMENT AND RANKING OF YOUR 25 CORE SKILLS AND THE CONNECTION TO WHAT THE JOB REQUIRES

A key phrase defining personal core skills in the description above is "the connection to what the job requires." It's not necessary or even practical to be highly developed in every skill. Development of a personal skill may not advance your career if it's not required in your current job. That's why it's important to know what skills the job requires. When you know that information, you can determine what skills need development and on what level.

When coaching your team member, be aware of what skills her job actually requires. When you see her report of the 25 core skills ranked for her, here are the questions to ask:

- Of the top seven core skills, which of these are required in your work? To what extent? Are you using these skills in your current job?
- Then review the following 18 Core Skills in the report and determine if and to what extent these skills are required in your team member's current job. Assess what skills would be valuable to develop further.

Of the 25 Core Skills we measure, some will be transferrable, such as:

- Time Mastery – prioritizing and completing tasks in order to deliver desired outcomes within allotted time frames.
- Resiliency – quick recovery from adversity.
- Personal Accountability – being answerable for personal actions.
- Teamwork – cooperating with others to meet objectives.
- Interpersonal Skills – effectively communicating and building rapport.

Other skills may be nice to develop, but perhaps not as necessary to be highly developed regarding your team member's current job, such as:

- Futuristic Thinking – imagining, envisioning, projecting, and/or creating what has not yet been actualized.
- Negotiation – listening to many points of view and facilitating agreements between two or more parties.
- Project Management – identifying and overseeing all resources, tasks, systems, and people to obtain results.

CASE IN POINT

In reviewing Debra's report before beginning a coaching relationship, I noticed her Time Management and Priority Management scores were in the bottom five. This was linked to her behavioral style, which indicated she's all about relationships. She can get the tasks done, but she tends to procrastinate and wait until the last minute to plan.

Since being promoted to vice president, it's critical that Debra gets a grip on managing her calendar, her projects, and her time. Her responsibilities are greater since she has a larger team, a bigger budget, and more stress. And that's not counting the stress she is most likely causing others by delaying tasks.

Improving her Time Management and Priority Management is a primary goal in working with Debra in a coaching relationship.

Appendix D

Understanding Your Acumen

UNDERSTANDING AND APPLYING EAGERNESS AND DEPTH OF DISCERNMENT FOR PROBLEM-SOLVING AND DECISION-MAKING

While behavior and drivers are about the person as well as the people they interact with, acumen is about the individual person. It measures how clearly you think, make decisions, and solve problems and is connected to two areas:

- How clearly a person sees the external world around them. This includes how clearly they see and understand people, tasks, and systems. When reviewing the "External Factors" section in the assessment report, you can discern what type of manager the person is. We'll know how well he understands other people, how clearly he sees what practical tasks need to be done, and how clearly he sees systems and rules.

- How clearly a person sees herself in the world. This includes the internal factors of her Sense of Self, Role Awareness, and Self-Direction. When reviewing the "Internal Factors" section in the assessment report, you can discern a person's confidence level and how she values herself, how clearly she sees her roles in life/work, and how clearly she sees her future. Is there a sense of hope for the future?

WHY MEASURE ACUMEN?

Two of the most interesting pieces of information that can be gleaned from this assessment are Role Clarity and Self-Direction. Everyone has multiple roles they play in life: career person, parent, daughter or son, sister or brother, friend, volunteer, etc. If a Role Awareness score is high, probably the Self-Direction score is also high. If you are clear on your roles and like your roles, then your hope and vision for the future are high.

If a Role Awareness score is low, it shows lack of clarity in some part of the person's life. If a person is starting a new job or taking on a large project, it's not unusual for this dimension to be a little lower. They probably don't have clarity on expectations, or they may be cautious while learning something new. It affects their future view, which is uncertain until they master this part of their life.

Earlier in this book, I mentioned that a person you are coaching will bring "who they are and everything that's going on in their life" with them to these sessions. When I see a Role Awareness score that's somewhat low, I explore the work environment first. If all seems solid there, I ask about home life. This is where the personal stories come up and where a person often struggles with how to handle the situation and perhaps even has confusion for their future.

When a group of people on a team all have low Role Awareness, the key leader needs to know.

CASE IN POINT

Some years ago, a current client recommended me to a CEO of a young, growing organization. John had recently taken over what started as a small family business but had taken root quickly. Soon John had a full team of leaders and multiple issues moving quickly.

John wanted to know more about himself, his leadership style, and what he needed to learn to grow as a person. He experienced our battery of assessments and learned a great deal about himself. I crafted a short coaching program for him, and he was fully engaged and motivated. The next phase was to assess his leadership team and help them grow and work well together too.

Now for the interesting part: Each of the eight key leaders had a low Role Awareness score! It seems things were moving so fast in this energetic, fast-growing company that they were all somewhat confused about who was to do what. They spent a lot of time "running around with a fire extinguisher putting out fires," they said.

Gathering data, I met with John and explained the situation, showing him the scores of his team in this one area. We discussed his vision and what he expected of each of the leaders in their current role. He thought he had communicated all this to his team, but said he apparently wasn't clear enough.

The very next day, John gathered his team and shared his vision and strategy once again, clarifying what he expected from each person and their role. This was a huge epiphany for John, and his quick action to communicate with his team and clarify roles saved immeasurable time and dollars, not to mention frustration and stress on the part of all the team members.

Appendix E

Unleashing Your Emotional Intelligence

THE FIVE HIERARCHICAL COMPETENCIES THAT BUILD STRONG RELATIONSHIPS AND HIGH LEVELS OF COLLABORATION REQUIRED IN LEADERSHIP – SELF-AWARENESS, SELF-REGULATION, MOTIVATION, EMPATHY, AND SOCIAL SKILLS

Many leaders are hired for their skills, yet they often derail because of lack of success with people. That's where emotional intelligence comes in. It's based on brain science and the two, small, almond-like groups of neurons called the amygdala. (Be careful, because those "creatures" hidden in your brain can hijack your emotions and your behavior before you know what happened! If you've ever said or done something so outrageous that you even shocked yourself, then you've been hijacked by your amygdala.)

The good news about emotional intelligence is that it can be learned and often increases as you mature. Now we'd like to think maturity is linked to age, but we all know allegedly mature people in their 60s or beyond who are not very mature. And conversely, we all know younger people who have a deep sense of maturity.

There are five competencies in emotional intelligence that are built on each other:

1. **Self-Awareness.**
    a. Recognizing feelings and emotions as they happen.
    b. Being aware of your moods and their effects on other people.
    c. Having a sound sense of self-worth and capabilities.
    d. Making realistic self-assessment of your strengths and limitations.
2. **Self-Regulation.**
    a. Controlling or redirecting your emotions and disruptive impulses and moods.
    b. Handling feelings appropriately (especially the big three – anger, anxiety, and sadness) and to soothe yourself and shake them off.
3. **Motivation.**
    a. Having a passion to work for reasons beyond money or status.
    b. Being driven to pursue goals with energy and persistence.
4. **Empathy.**
    a. Recognizing and understanding the emotional makeup of other people.
    b. Sensing unstated feelings of others and articulating them.
    c. Serving and showing compassion.
5. **Social Skills.**
    a. Having the ability to form a web of relationships and to create and lead teams.
    b. Leading and managing change effectively.

c. Inspiring others with a compelling vision.

d. Coaching through feedback and guidance.

WHY IS EMOTIONAL INTELLIGENCE SO IMPORTANT?

IQ contributes, at best, about 30 percent of the factors that determine success. Two-thirds of the abilities that set star performers apart are based on EQ.

– Daniel Goleman in his book *Emotional Intelligence: Why it Can Matter More than IQ*

90% of abilities that set star performing CEOs apart are based on EQ.

– Daniel Goleman in his book *Focus: The Hidden Driver of Excellence*

CASE IN POINT

The first words I heard when I picked up the phone were, "Help! This is Gail, and I need your help again!"

Gail was the vice president of human resources of a large health system with multiple facilities around the country. She went on to explain that she was having some challenges with Peter, one of her CEOs. He was making his numbers, and in fact his was the most profitable hospital in the group, his census was good, and his facility was on target with its building expansion. However, his lack of people skills was killing him; he just didn't seem to understand relationships and how to interact with people in a professional way. While he was very outgoing and friendly, he didn't seem to be able to control his comments and his moods. And on and on she went.

My first question was, "How did he respond when you brought this up to him?" I heard nothing but silence on the other end of the line. OK, I thought, no one has talked to him about this. This is not unusual. Many leaders avoid this kind of discussion, in part because they don't have the skills to deal with it. Remember that what you permit, you promote. Not getting feedback on his behavior, Peter never thought there was a problem.

This seemed to be an emotional intelligence issue, so I agreed to talk with Peter and see if he was coachable and willing to understand and develop his EQ.

When I first met Peter his charm and bright smile made him immediately likeable. He seemed eager to grow and discover what behavior was derailing him and fix it. His positive attitude made him a perfect candidate to understand and develop his emotional intelligence.

The first step was to have him experience the full battery of executive assessments, including the EQ assessment to measure the five competencies. Peter's EQ scores were all very low except Motivation, which was actually high. His low Self-Awareness score played out in his behavior. He really didn't see how he was coming across to others. Since you can't change or adjust what you don't know, it followed that his Self-Regulation suffered, too.

So that's where coaching started. Because he had little idea of the effects of his behavior, his first assignment was to journal each day to increase awareness of how he came across to others. He was to note how people responded to him by watching body language and listening with attention to what they were saying. Once he was aware of his communication and how people received it, he was able to begin to adjust and regulate his comments.

Peter had two questions to ask himself at the end of every day: 1. What went well today? 2. What could I have done differently? These questions anchored his success and brought greater awareness to how he could handle a similar situation next time.

Peter was faithful in his practice and feedback to me. Gradually over the course of several months, his Self-Awareness grew as did his Self-Regulation. He was more conscious of thinking before he spoke, and he was getting more positive feedback from his team.

With continued practice and regular coaching, nearly a year later Peter repeated the EQ assessment. Scores change slowly in this body of knowledge, but his score on Self-Awareness and Self-Regulation increased by three points, which is a big jump. Remember that motivation was never an issue for him.

And with greater Self-Awareness and Self-Regulation, Peter was becoming more adept at building better professional relationships and leading and communicating with his team. I still talk with Peter periodically. He's continuing to practice what he learned from this experience, he has grown as a person, and his career has taken many new positive turns.

PURCHASING OR BECOMING TRAINED IN OUR ASSESSMENTS

The assessments and the five sciences discussed here have been researched and developed by Target Training International, Ltd./TTI Success Insights of Scottsdale,

Arizona. The assessments are validated and reliable, and with training, they are easy to administer and interpret. Information about the assessments included in this book is used with permission of TTI. For further information in understanding DISC, the following reference is available: *The Universal Language DISC: A Reference Manual* by Bill J. Bonnstetter and Judy I. Suiter.

To be trained to use any of these assessments with your team or to invite me to work with your leaders, email me at elizabeth@tweedjeffries.com.

Acknowledgements

To these precious people in my life, I humbly offer up the two most profound words I know: **Thank You!**

Bill McGrane for teaching me the skill of people reading and for modeling TUA (total unconditional acceptance). You asked and listened and pushed and hugged and expected more from me than I would have ever asked of myself. The impact you made on my life and my work is immeasurable. You left us far too soon, Bill. I'll see you in heaven for sure.

Shawn Kent Hayashi for all the roles you play in my life: a forever friend, a learning partner, a soul sister, a daughter, and a mentee who quickly grew far beyond me. Thank you for reviewing my manuscript. Your suggestions were right on target. I love you with TUA.

Cathy Fyock for our conversation at dinner where you asked me, "Why haven't you written another book? You know so much about executive coaching; you need to share it with others." Thank you for being my book coach, reviewing the manuscript several times, and setting the stage where I could write it in three weeks. You were the spark that got me started!

My Summit Sisters: Glenna Salsbury, Naomi Rhode, Liz Curtis Higgs and Gail Wenos for patiently listening to my book concept and encouraging me to read a whole chapter to you and then brainstorm titles. Talk about unconditional love! You four have blessed me for over 25 years with your wisdom, laughter, friendship, and how you model the love of Christ.

Dee Ann Campbell who started me on the path of coaching nearly 20 years ago. You never knew how far your reach would extend all these years later.

Bill Bonnstetter, the late chairman of Target Training International, Ltd./TTI Success Insights, the researchers and developers of the validated assessments I'm certified in and have been using for nearly 20 years. My coaching practice wouldn't be what it is today without these five sciences. We miss you, Bill, but your legacy lives on in the millions of people you've served through these assessments.

Dr. Deb Clary and Michael Tate for reviewing the manuscript and challenging me to look at an idea differently. I made changes because of your great suggestions.

Each and every client I've had the privilege of coaching these past 20 years. I'm humbled that you opened your mind and your heart to me, listened to my sometimes-pretty-deep questions, and took action on ideas and celebrated new and exciting outcomes. You were my teachers too, and I learned much from you. I'm beyond blessed to have been a small part of your life and your work.

Stephen Tweed, my beloved husband, my encourager, my business partner, my logical, stable thinker who balances the impulsive, emotional side of me. Thank you for reading and rereading the manuscript and rereading it yet again. With each of our zillion conversations, you gave me great insights to make this book better. Thank you for always listening and smiling softly with understanding when I tell you how much I love my work and my clients. You are my anchor and my forever love.

My Lord God who inspired every word in this book. Only through You, Lord, was it possible the manuscript was written in three weeks. To you be the glory!

About the Author

Elizabeth Jeffries
Hall of Fame Speaker,
Executive Leadership
Coach, Author

Elizabeth Jeffries, is an award-winning professional speaker, executive leadership coach, and author. She works with CEOs, C-suite executives, and physician leaders who want to enliven their organizations, select and onboard great people, and turn all their leaders into high performers!

Her clients include health systems, post-acute health care organizations, service businesses, churches, and professional associations.

An experienced coach to scores of high-level leaders, Elizabeth is a master in asking the tough questions and processing leaders to think bigger, work differently, and break through to new outcomes. She's a truth-teller and powerful facilitator of executive and board retreats, skillfully engaging leaders at their highest level of need.

Whether the challenge is the organization, the team, or the individual executive, Elizabeth's skills as a process coach will uncover the gaps blocking their success journey. Armed with a Solutions Toolkit™ she comes prepared with unbiased, objective, validated assessments, and surveys that will open communication, create awareness, and move leaders to take action for new results.

A member of the elite Council of Peers Award for Excellence (CPAE) Speaker Hall of Fame, Elizabeth presents keynote speeches and interactive learning events at corporate meetings and association conferences. She has addressed over one million people in more than 4,000 presentations in the past three decades.

Learn more about Elizabeth and her services at www.tweedjeffries.com.

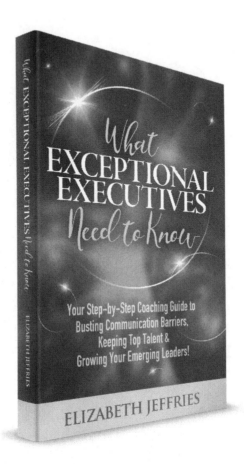

To receive training on any of these assessments discussed in this book or to invite Elizabeth Jeffries to work with your leaders, contact her at elizabeth@tweedjeffries.com.

Made in the USA
Lexington, KY
06 February 2018